ENHANCING GENDER EQUALITY IN INFRASTRUCTURE DEVELOPMENT

THEORIES OF CHANGE, INDICATORS, AND SECTOR STRATEGIES

DECEMBER 2023

ASIAN DEVELOPMENT BANK

ADB

ISBN 978-92-9270-563-3 (print); 978-92-9270-564-0 (electronic); 978-92-9270-565-7 (ebook)
Publication Stock No. TCS230608-2
DOI: http://dx.doi.org/10.22617/TCS230608-2

The views expressed in this publication are those of the authors and do not necessarily reflect the views and policies of the Asian Development Bank (ADB) or its Board of Governors or the governments they represent.

ADB does not guarantee the accuracy of the data included in this publication and accepts no responsibility for any consequence of their use. The mention of specific companies or products of manufacturers does not imply that they are endorsed or recommended by ADB in preference to others of a similar nature that are not mentioned.

By making any designation of or reference to a particular territory or geographic area, or by using the term "country" in this publication, ADB does not intend to make any judgments as to the legal or other status of any territory or area.

Corrigenda to ADB publications may be found at http://www.adb.org/publications/corrigenda.

Notes:
In this publication, "$" refers to United States dollars and "€" refers to European euro.
ADB recognizes "USA" as the United States.

Cover design by Patrick Francisco.

On the cover: **Shaping Progress.** *On the left*, a vibrant image captures engineers, men and women in hard hats, actively contributing at the Lahendong Geothermal Plant in Manado, Indonesia. *On the top right*, the empowering scene features an all-woman team at the Narangi Substation in eastern Guwahati, India, illustrating the transformative role of gender diversity in infrastructure.

CONTENTS

TABLES, FIGURES, AND BOXES

FOREWORD

To make infrastructure work for everyone, there needs to be a critical shift in how it is designed, delivered, and managed. The absence of affordable, convenient, and secure infrastructure services impedes the access of women to economic, political, and social opportunities and access to educational and health-care services. Achieving gender equality and empowering women is not just a moral imperative but is also a strategic necessity for sustainable infrastructure development. This understanding is gaining traction and finding resonance in key policy frameworks like the G20 Principles for Quality Infrastructure Investment, particularly Principle 5 on "Integrating Social Considerations in Infrastructure Investment." Embedding the perspectives and needs of women and girls within infrastructure projects is crucial for promoting holistic economic development.

Recognizing that a significant percentage of its investment portfolio comprises investment in infrastructure, the Asian Development Bank (ADB) commits resolutely to addressing gender disparities, especially within infrastructure development. The ADB Strategy 2030 emphasizes the pivotal role of gender equality in driving socioeconomic progress across Asia and the Pacific. This commitment manifests as one of the central operational priorities. Across five strategic pillars—economic empowerment, human development, decision-making and leadership, reduced time poverty of women, and resilience to external shocks—ADB is firmly dedicated to accelerating gender equality outcomes in the region.

This is actualized through ADB's commitment to incorporating gender-inclusive project designs in 75% of its sovereign and nonsovereign operations by 2030. This commitment aligns seamlessly with the 2030 Agenda for Sustainable Development, which unites ADB and its developing member countries in their support for gender equality and women's empowerment. This dedication extends beyond the confines of Sustainable Development Goal (SDG) 5, encompassing the broader spectrum of SDGs through the integration of gender-related targets and indicators. ADB's emphasis on measuring gender equality outcomes remains consistent within its operations. Gender performance indicators are integrated into infrastructure projects to optimize benefits for women and girls.

This report responds to the need for more analysis and concrete data on how gender-responsive infrastructure can lead to women's empowerment, embodying ADB's commitment to assessing the gender impact of quality infrastructure investments. It delves beyond immediate gains for women and girls, exploring the strategic potential: increased decision-making capacity, improved health, enhanced income, transformed social norms, and a more equitable societal environment.

Despite progress, the journey toward gender equality in infrastructure projects remains a dynamic process. Challenges persist, opportunities evolve, and the social and cultural norms that underpin exclusion take time to change. This report does not claim to provide an exhaustive guide but endeavors to provide a starting point to inspire action. The examples of project features to enhance the impact on gender equality and women's empowerment presented in this report are intended as foundations upon which infrastructure projects can be built. More work is needed to transform aspirations into realities. This report hopes to catalyze change, paving the way for infrastructure projects that genuinely empower and include all people regardless of gender.

Bruno Carrasco
Director General
Climate Change and Sustainable Development Department
Asian Development Bank

ACKNOWLEDGMENTS

This report is prepared under the technical assistance project *Support to the Implementation of Strategy 2030 Operational Plans*. Prabhjot Khan, social development specialist (gender and development) with the Asian Development Bank (ADB) Climate Change and Sustainable Development Department (CCSD), led the development of the publication with support from Maria Jeunessa D. Sto Nino, national results management specialist; and Alih Faisal Pimentel Abdul, coordinating consultant. Ann Mushayt W. Alemania, operations analyst; and Ma. Celia A. Guzon, senior operations assistant (gender and development), both with CCSD, provided administrative support. Faraz Hassan and Chris Hearle of Social Development Direct prepared the draft. Melanie Kelleher copyedited the report, while Joe Mark Ganaban provided the layout.

The publication benefited from peer reviewers Katja Jobes and Tasneem Salam, both independent experts/consultants; and from the following ADB staff: Priyantha Wijayatunga, senior director, Energy Sector Office; Lara Arjan, urban development specialist, Water and Urban Development Sector Office; David Shelton, senior transport specialist (road safety), Transport Sector Office; and many ADB staff members who provided valuable comments and inputs to this publication. Special mention to Malika Shagazatova, senior social development specialist (gender and development), CCSD, who led the initial development phase of this publication, setting the foundation for its content.

Special thanks to Samantha Hung, director of the Gender Equality Division with CCSD for overall support and guidance throughout the process.

ABBREVIATIONS

ADB	Asian Development Bank
CBDM	Community-Based Disaster Management Flood and Earthquake Preparedness and Response Programme (Bangladesh)
DMF	design and monitoring framework
GMPL	GreenCell Mobility Private Limited
M&E	monitoring and evaluation
SDG	Sustainable Development Goal
SRSP	Sarhad Rural Support Programme (Bangladesh)
STEM	science, technology, engineering, and mathematics
TOC	theory of change

1 INTRODUCTION

This document contains theories of change (TOCs) and indicators to enable gender-inclusive development in four key sectors of infrastructure investment by the Asian Development Bank (ADB). It was designed to function as a point of reference for the development of infrastructure investment projects and programs with enhanced gender equality outcomes. The purpose of the four TOCs is to identify activities, components, and critical features of infrastructure projects that can enhance gender equality and women's empowerment outcomes and to articulate what needs to be measured to monitor and evaluate these results. These TOCs are a starting point to enable ADB teams developing projects in ADB developing member countries to adapt gender-related features relevant to their key objectives, outputs, and outcomes of specific projects. This document—including the TOCs and examples of project features—focuses on creating a positive impact rather than the environmental and social risk management of projects. ADB staff should consider suggestions in this document alongside gender considerations in risk management approaches.

This report developed the theories of change from

(i) desk reviews of literature, published research, and case studies to identify how activities and project outputs lead to outcomes in gender equality and women's empowerment;

(ii) desk reviews of ADB policies and guidance on gender equality and results monitoring including Operational Priority 2: Accelerating Progress in Gender Equality and the ADB Design and Monitoring Framework (DMF); and

(iii) a co-creation workshop and collaboration with the ADB Gender and Urban teams.

This study intends to inform a measurement framework to capture outputs and outcomes that ADB staff can use to select suitable indicators and monitoring tools for evaluating outcomes on gender equality at project completion. The broader intention is to facilitate and promote more *gender equity theme*-categorized projects in the ADB portfolio. The measurement framework will build on indicators and measurement activities undertaken by ADB and highlight where additional data collection is needed.

The TOCs are intended to be used as a starting point for ADB to review and adapt on an ongoing basis, while also providing a shared understanding of how ADB investments can lead to gender equality and women's empowerment-related outcomes. They are not intended to be fully comprehensive but rather to provide key indicative avenues or "pathways" for change so that they can inform project-by-project gender entry points, analysis, and identification of suitable gender inclusion measures, ultimately enhancing the gender impacts of ADB infrastructure investments.

Structure of the Paper

This paper **outlines the case** for why investing in gender equality and women's empowerment as part of infrastructure projects makes sense, particularly the business case (section 2). Some examples presented are gender relations, social norms, and attitudes that systematically disadvantage women and girls and how these link to infrastructure. These serve to contextualize the problem statements and selected outcomes utilized in the TOCs. Opportunities are highlighted in a business case to provide context for engagement with stakeholders and for raising awareness of addressing gender equality and women's empowerment as critical factors in the achievement of sustainable and impactful financial investments.

The paper then presents a series of **key considerations and entry points in infrastructure programs** (section 3) for gender inclusion and addressing gender equality and women's empowerment. These key considerations and entry points are designed to sit alongside the theory of change diagrams and illustrate the kind of gender-responsive features that could be incorporated into activities. This section aims to inform project design and outline what might be involved to achieve desired outcomes in gender equality, including crosscutting good practices in mainstreaming gender equality in infrastructure projects.

Section 4 presents **four sector theory of change diagrams for (i) urban development, (ii) transport, (iii) water, sanitation, and hygiene (WASH),** and **(iv) energy**. These TOCs are designed to provide examples of how infrastructure projects can lead to positive outcomes in gender equality and women's empowerment. Risks and assumptions are outlined alongside the diagrams.

Section 5 presents a set of **key recommendations**, with a focus on summarizing how information presented in this paper can be used.

A menu of **example indicators for outputs and outcomes** featured in the theory of change diagrams is provided in Annex 1. Annex 2 provides a **set of case studies from ADB to illustrate the approaches mentioned in this paper**.

2 WHY ADDRESS GENDER EQUALITY AND WOMEN AND GIRLS' INCLUSION IN INFRASTRUCTURE PROJECTS?

2.1 How Inadequate Infrastructure Disproportionately Impacts Women and Girls

The benefits of infrastructure investments are not distributed equally between women and men. This discrepancy arises because of the assignment of roles, expectations, and levels of decision-making for women and men within society. Consequently, women and girls may experience reduced opportunities to fully enjoy the advantages brought about by infrastructure development compared to men and boys (ADB 2019). It is crucial to acknowledge the systematic disadvantages and exclusions faced by women and girls because of gender relations, social norms, attitudes, and behaviors when preparing infrastructure projects. Failing to consider these factors can result in the creation of a "gender-blind" infrastructure, exacerbating and perpetuating inequality. Furthermore, such oversight hampers the ability of women and girls to contribute equally to society and hinders their access to safety, opportunities, and equal rights (Menon 2019). To contextualize the theories of change in this paper—particularly the problem statements within them—Table 1 highlights examples of the ways women and girls can be excluded or disadvantaged and how infrastructure projects can address these challenges.

Table 1: How the Exclusion of Women and Girls Links to Infrastructure

Gender Relations and Social Norms, Attitudes, and Behaviors	Examples of How This Impacts Women and Girls	Infrastructure Related Opportunity
The gendered division of labor means women and girls are still largely responsible for most domestic chores, childcare, and caregiving, making them "time poor."	Inadequate sanitation in India costs the economy $213 million annually because of time lost at work and school as the result of illness and caring for the sick, duties for which women are often responsible. Women are less likely to own private vehicles compared to men, leading them to depend more on public transportation and bear a disproportionate burden of the opportunity costs associated with inadequate or expensive transportation.	Improvements in transportation infrastructure, or improved access to utilities and resources—including pipe-borne water and electricity—can have significant knock-on effects on women's physical mobility and time savings, which can enable access to more, higher paying jobs for women and new opportunities for business expansion and productivity for women-owned businesses.

continued on next page

Table 1 *continued*

Gender Relations and Social Norms, Attitudes, and Behaviors	Examples of How This Impacts Women and Girls	Infrastructure Related Opportunity
Women and girls systematically have fewer opportunities and face more barriers to economic and income earning opportunities.	Globally, women continue to have lower workforce participation compared to men, are more prone to unemployment than men, often find themselves in less secure and informal jobs, and are paid less than men. In addition, women generally have less job security or social protections than men. Only 1% of the public procurement sector is accounted for by businesses owned by women. These enterprises frequently cite insufficient knowledge about opportunities and criteria, intricate processes, and rigorous financial and qualification prerequisites as obstacles in securing public contracts.	Transport services and urban planning that meet the needs of women can lead to reduced time poverty and increased access to economic opportunities including higher paid jobs and markets. The construction of new infrastructure facilities yields new opportunities for labor market participation. Investments in infrastructure can boost the productivity of businesses and enhance their connections with customers and suppliers. Such enhancements can lead to higher and steadier earnings for workers, including women, who are more likely than men to operate home-based businesses and manage enterprises in informal settlements, which often lack fundamental amenities like water and energy.
Women are at additional risk of violence and harassment in infrastructure settings, which can include harassment and violence in public spaces; unsafe public transportation; or assaults while using and traveling to or from water and sanitary facilities.	One in three women experience some form of physical and sexual violence in their lifetime (Fraser et al., 2017). This violence—along with the constant threat of it—hinders economic progress in urban areas, disproportionately affecting women's freedom of movement, access to public spaces, educational opportunities, economic engagement, political participation, and pursuit of higher-paying or secure jobs. For instance, in Port Moresby, Papua New Guinea, a study revealed that more than 90% of women and girls faced some form of violence while using public transportation, including buses, bus stops, walking to and from stops, and taxis.	Better urban and transport planning; representation of women and girls; and safety-related policies and procedures in the development and operation of infrastructure have the potential to create safe, inclusive, and well planned public spaces, urban services, and transport which can reduce violence and harassment that women and girls face and increase access to economic opportunities.
The infrastructure sector is still predominantly male-dominated, leading to assumptions that infrastructure is gender-neutral.	Estimates suggest that in the infrastructure sector, just 2% of CEOs and 9% of senior positions are filled by women. Women hold 13% of mid-level roles and 22% of junior roles. This pattern holds for utility companies as well, where women represent 22% of the workforce. One study found that in the water, sanitation, and hygiene sector, women professionals made up less than 17% of the labor force.	Infrastructure investments can catalyze measures such as targeted human resource policies, recruitment and retention practices, targets, and shifting cultural norms to enhance representation and quality employment of women in sectors related to infrastructure design and construction.

continued on next page

Table 1 *continued*

Gender Relations and Social Norms, Attitudes, and Behaviors	Examples of How This Impacts Women and Girls	Infrastructure Related Opportunity
Discriminatory and patriarchal laws, regulations, and customs prevent women's access to and ownership of key assets like land.	Globally, women account for only 21% of all house owners (OECD, 2019). Women's property rights are limited in two-thirds of the world's economies. In the Pacific region, land and homeownership remains predominantly clan based and rests with men, preventing women from being registered owners.	Strong property rights and enhanced access to affordable housing can increase women's financial security and enable women to leverage assets for economic gain or for the collateral needed to start and grow a business.
Women tend to have less access to knowledge and information on impending weather events and how to prepare—or are less able to flee to safety—during a disaster because of care responsibilities.	Women are 14 times more likely to die or be injured during a disaster than men as they face additional barriers to resources and information and are often less able to evacuate in emergencies because of additional care. Responsibilities and social restrictions on movement. In 1991, during the cyclone disasters in Bangladesh, 90% of the 140,000 people who died were women.	Integrating gender equality considerations and involving women and girls in the design of disaster resilience measures and infrastructure, such as shelters or early warning systems, as well as in disaster recovery plans, can enhance the reach and impact of these measures, while mitigating the disproportionate harm experienced by women and girls because of disasters and climate change.

Sources: 2X Climate Finance Taskforce. 2021. *Ways to Gender-Smart Climate Finance: Sustainable Cities*.
Asian Development Bank (ADB). 2013a. *Gender Tool Kit: Transport. Manila*.
ADB. 2015a. *Balancing the burden? Desk review of women's time poverty and infrastructure in Asia and the Pacific*. Manila.
British International Investment. n.d. *Sector Profiles: Infrastructure*.
E. Fraser et al. 2017. *Violence against Women and Girls, Infrastructure and Cities: Briefing Paper*. Government of the United Kingdom, Infrastructure and Cities for Economic Development (ICED).
International Trade Centre. 2020. *Making Public Procurement Work for Women*. Geneva.
International Union for Conservation of Nature (n.d.) *Disaster and Gender Statistics*.
Organisation for Economic Co-operation and Development (OECD). 2019. *Sustainable Connectivity: Closing the Gender Gap in Infrastructure*. *OECD Environment Policy Paper* No. 15.
Office of the United Nations High Commissioner for Human Rights. 2012. *Women and the Right to Adequate Housing*.
The Solutions Lab. 2020. *Gender-Responsive Infrastructure: Thematic Brief*.
UN Women Fiji. 2014. *Why is climate change a gender issue*?
UN Women. 2014. *Making markets safer for women vendors in Papua New Guinea*. News story. 14 April.
UN Women. (n.d.) *Facts and Figures: Economic Empowerment*.
G. Morgan et al. 2020. *Infrastructure for gender equality and the empowerment of women*. Copenhagen, Denmark: UNOPS.
World Bank. 2021. *Women, Business and the Law 2021*. Washington, DC: World Bank.

While Table 1 is not comprehensive, it highlights how adopting a gender-blind infrastructure is a missed opportunity and could end up exacerbating inequalities. Conversely, infrastructure projects present a key opportunity to address barriers to gender equality and women's empowerment.

2.2 The Business Case

Accelerating progress in gender equality—including in infrastructure settings—is a key part of achieving the SDGs as well as being part of ADB's Strategy 2030. There is a strong business case for addressing gender equality and women's empowerment as part of infrastructure investments. This section aims to provide ADB and project staff with a clear evidence-based rationale and broad contextual analysis for stakeholder engagement on the added value of incorporating gender inclusion across ADB's investment portfolio. The business case sets out opportunities from the use of the infrastructure itself as well as employment and supply chain impact.

Key Opportunities: Urban Development

More than 80% of the global GDP is generated in cities. Women's inclusion in urban planning and infrastructure development enables meaningful participation by women in urban life and directly leads to economic growth. Ignoring women's needs limits the productivity of urban populations.

- Policies targeting women's economic empowerment can contribute $28 trillion (a 26% increase) to global GDP in a decade (McKinsey 2015).
- The OECD estimates that applying a gender lens to infrastructure development would increase the total GDP of its member states by 2.5% until 2050 (The Solutions Lab 2020; Sustainable Infrastructure Tool Navigator, n.d.).
- Closing the gender labor gap would allow for 22.5% economic growth according to the International Monetary Fund (Yepez 2023).

Urban areas meeting women's needs as well as men's are more competitive, attract businesses, and support more equitable and sustainable economic growth.

- Addressing mobility constraints and safety concerns increases women's movement, boosting footfall for markets and commercial activities (Arup 2022). For example, in Port Moresby, Papua New Guinea, the high prevalence of sexual violence in market spaces (affecting 55% of women) meant that local and foreign customers stopped going to the markets (UN Women 2014).
- Adequate street lighting increases the hours women and men can safely move around the city and access jobs. The cost to the world economy of violence against women and girls is estimated to be $8 trillion annually (Hoeffler and Fearon 2015).

Improved urban infrastructure reduces women's time poverty, unlocking a ready female labor force in urban centers.

- Locating transport near key services such as schools, health centers, markets, and commercial centers reduces travel time for women and men so they can juggle both income earning and caring responsibilities. In developing countries, lack of access to and the safety of transport reduces the probability of women's participation in the labor force by 16.5% (ILO 2017).
- In Puebla, Mexico, long commute times were found to deter women from better job opportunities in the city center (Libertun de Duren 2017; World Bank 2015).

Addressing the housing needs of women and promoting homeownership promotes economic activities.

- Secure and affordable housing boosts the productivity of home-based workers, who are mainly women (F. Bonnet et al. 2021).
- Incorporating women's needs in housing location, affordability, and design improves the productivity of women entrepreneurs and informal enterprises (Mohun and Biswas 2016).
- Landownership and land title in a woman's name means it can be used as collateral for access to e.g., finance which can support women's home-based income generation (Landesa 2012).
- Adequate water and sanitation enhance profitability and growth for home-based workers and street vendors as less time is spent gathering water (a task commonly assigned to women)

or traveling to sanitation facilities and more time can be spent on productive activities (Roever 2014; WIEGO 2019). A lack of water, sanitation, and hygiene (WASH) facilities was found to reduce earnings by up to 20% for women street vendors who need to leave their stalls unattended for extended periods to access WASH facilities far away (Carr 2019).

- Women's inclusion in municipal leadership and technical planning roles improves resilience, innovation, and infrastructure quality as they can respond to the differentiated needs of women as well as men. Only 20% of city mayors globally are women (IFC 2020).
- More women employees in transport companies enhance service delivery, safety perceptions, ridership, and operating efficiencies, as they better understand the needs and priorities of women customers and provide a sense of security when visible to other women in transport settings (ADB 2013a; European Commission 2018).

Increasing women's labor force participation boosts financial returns, innovation, and sustainability, and can provide cities with a skilled workforce.

- Evidence demonstrates that inclusive business cultures appealing to women can increase profitability, talent attraction, and retention because of having diverse ideas and experiences (Yepez 2023).
- Diversity in teams leads to new and innovative solutions because of diverse experiences and ideas helping services, for example, appeal to or meet the needs of women customers (Giannelos et al. 2018).
- Evidence shows that companies with more women on boards have higher environmental ratings, as they tend to be open to adopting green practices (FP Analytics 2020).

Key Opportunities: Transport

Incorporating women's safety and travel needs is an important part of increasing ridership and revenues generated from transport investments.

- Safe, attractive, convenient, and affordable transport systems designed for the travel requirements of girls and women as well as men and boys (who tend to have different travel needs) increase the customer base and ridership and therefore the revenue and emissions savings bringing benefits for all (Peters 2013).
- Neglecting women's safety concerns in public transport design can result in lower usage and inaccurate commercial forecasts (ADB 2013a).
- Women have been found to be more willing to adopt green travel solutions and public transport, making them a crucial market for green growth in cities (European Parliament 2012; Where Women Work 2022). Research suggests that if men began traveling as women do, emissions would be reduced by 18% (Lind 2020).

Safety concerns are a primary factor in women's choices around transportation (ADB 2013a; ADB 2015). Failing to account for them can lead to inaccuracies in feasibility and commercial forecasts for transport programs.

- Personal security is a primary factor for women workers in choosing their daily commute mode, especially for lower-income women (ADB 2013a; Campbell et al. 2016).

⊘ Commercial dimensions of women's use of proposed transport infrastructure and their latent demand are frequently neglected in feasibility studies, including their willingness and ability to pay for special services, leading to inaccurate commercial forecasts and missed opportunities for businesses and women themselves (Peters 2013).

Transport investments that plan for women's distinct needs can boost economic activity and strengthen supply chains.

⊘ Transport investments supporting women's mobility and links to commercial centers and markets improve supply chain efficiencies for home-based workers, women entrepreneurs, and market traders who rely on regular travel to buy supplies, negotiate orders, and sell goods (Chen 2014; Vanek et al. 2014).

Including women in infrastructure design and construction teams improves infrastructure quality and reduces costs.

⊘ The World Bank-funded Decentralized Rural Transport Project in Peru employed 27% women during construction which resulted in improved access, economic opportunities, and increased overall project performance (Munoz-Raskin et al. 2017).
⊘ Women's presence in road committees contributed to transparency in managing income, effective payment negotiations, and responsible quality control (World Bank 2010).

Key Opportunities: Water, Sanitation, and Hygiene

Enhancing access to safe, clean drinking water reduces time spent on collecting water, a burden that disproportionately falls on women and girls because of the gender division of labor.

⊘ Hygienic sanitation infrastructure is crucial for women's health, privacy, and safety. Easily accessible washing and drinking water benefits everyone and removes the need to walk long distances, a burden often placed on girls and women (Arup 2022).
⊘ Access to water services improves women's socioeconomic status by reducing time spent on household chores such as gathering water and health risks associated with unsafe water (UN Water 2006; WHO and UNICEF 2017).

Investing in WASH targeted at women can unlock new revenue streams and increase returns.

⊘ Infrastructure investments targeting low-income women unlock new revenue streams, as the demand for safe water and sanitation is high among both urban and rural women. One study from South Africa found that female-headed households were more inclined to pay via meter than a flat rate for water consumption (Akinyemi et al. 2018).
⊘ Investing in water and sanitation for unserved populations, including women and men, yields substantial economic gains, with estimated returns of $3 to $6 for every dollar invested (M. Grant et al. 2017; Hutton 2015).

Poor sanitation and associated health impacts on women and girls reduces economic potential.

- Poor sanitation leads to significant economic losses, impacting women's economic resilience and girls' education and potential. For example, time lost at school because of girls' absenteeism because of inadequate menstrual hygiene management facilities reduces their education and economic potential (Jasper et al. 2012; UN 2015).

Involving women in municipal service delivery and water governance leads to enhanced performance of companies and better water related outcomes.

- Involving more women in municipal service delivery enhances outcomes for all, with examples including increased drinking water projects in areas with women-led councils, and more effective water projects that include women in the workforce (Adams and Sorkin 2016; ADB 2015a; UN Women 2011; WSUP 2019).
- Women's involvement in water supply systems design and maintenance results in user-friendly designs and improved customer satisfaction (IFC 2019; Thompson et al. 2017).
- Increasing gender diversity in the water sector workforce enhances financial performance, innovation, efficiency, and customer relations of water utilities (World Bank 2019).
- Women's participation in water committees improves water management and sustainability, promoting socially inclusive, environmentally sustainable, and economically beneficial water practices (Thompson et al. 2017).

Key Opportunities: Energy

Enhancing women's access to electricity can increase female labor force participation.

- Access to gas, electricity, and labor-saving devices can reduce time spent on unpaid care and domestic chores which disproportionately impact girls and women. A reduction in unpaid care work by 2 hours is associated with a 10% increase in the women's labor force participation rate, while electrification in South Africa led to a 13.5% rise in female employment (Dinkelman 2011; Hislop 2021).
- Access to modern energy services reduces the time and effort spent on household chores and health risks, enabling women to invest in productive activities like leisure, education, health, and entrepreneurship (S. Habtezion 2012).
- Affordable and accessible electricity at home increases women's likelihood and ability to establish and grow home-based businesses (Mohun and Biswas 2016; O'Dell et al. 2014).

Recognizing women as an important market segment for energy and utility companies leads to enhanced financial viability.

- Women have a significant role in lighting purchase decisions and are responsible for 40% of these decisions (Alstone et al. 2011).
- Encouraging women's productive use of electricity—including affordable financing for energy-efficient appliances—enhances the financial viability of utilities (ESMP 2018).

Employing more women can lead to increased sales of energy products, including to women customers because of increased familiarity with productive energy use.

- ⮞ Women possess skills and knowledge for companies to capitalize on energy opportunities, particularly as women are the primary energy users and managers with extensive social networks (International Finance Corporation 2018).
- ⮞ Women's sales of clean stoves were 3 times higher than men's in Kenya, with women's customers reporting a better understanding of the products and their usage (Shankar et al. 2021).
- ⮞ Manufacturers of improved cookstoves experienced rapid sales growth (30%–300%) because of women's involvement in business operations (Business and Sustainable Development Commission 2017).
- ⮞ Women as energy sales agents can access untapped female markets, contributing to scaling distribution and building trust (UNEP 2020).
- ⮞ Involving women entrepreneurs in the supply chain increased sales of off-grid solutions by 85%, particularly in last mile markets (Shell Foundation 2018).

3 KEY CONSIDERATIONS AND ENTRY POINTS IN INTEGRATING GENDER INTO INFRASTRUCTURE PROJECTS

There are key entry points for integrating gender equality considerations into infrastructure projects. These entry points are designed to complement and provide context to the theory of change diagrams in section 4. They provide examples of specific project features that can be incorporated into activities outlined in the theory of change. This section draws on literature, evidence, and case studies to frame and present good practice on gender inclusion. While entry points can be considered or categorized in different ways, here the entry points have been developed around key needs (e.g., affordability), project development tools (e.g., urban planning guidelines), and women's representation. Further details are available in section 4.4 about the interrelation of different project features and how they lead to change.

3.1 Key Considerations in Mainstreaming Gender Equality and Women's Empowerment

ADB project teams should consider several crosscutting issues when designing infrastructure projects, which provide important contexts for entry points.

(i) **Entry points and activities exist on a spectrum in terms of the scale of impact they could have.** Infrastructure project features or entry points can vary in the level of impact and the extent to which they address systemic barriers to gender equality. Certain approaches can be very beneficial but will not change underlying cause–effect relationships (e.g., the design of transport systems that reflect travel patterns of women); others may lead to a sustainable impact on gender equality and women's economic empowerment (e.g., increasing skills, income earning, and employment opportunities for women and girls). Some project features may shift institutional, organizational, cultural, and societal norms, attitudes, and behaviors that discriminate and disadvantage females and that contribute to gender-based violence and harassment. It is important to be aware of the kinds of changes to gender equality an intervention might bring. To reflect this, the impact could be understood at three levels in terms of gender equality and women's economic empowerment.[1] These are as follows:

---

[1] The analytical framework draws on the work of Caroline Moser (2016). In collaboration with Social Development Direct, it was developed for the Infrastructure and Cites for Economic Development Programme (ICED) funded by the United Kingdom government.

(a) **Basic needs and priorities.** This includes addressing access and affordability to basic infrastructure and services for women and girls. This is necessary but insufficient and is a first step to help reduce things such as the drudgery and time poverty associated with care giving and/or domestic responsibilities.

(b) **Empowerment.** This relates to increasing women's skills, income earning, and employment opportunities, including for home-based, unskilled, skilled, and technical roles. It also includes increasing decision-making leadership and management roles for women; both on the demand side of infrastructure (i.e., for end users and/or female clients and customers) and the supply side (i.e., within municipal authorities, utility companies, and infrastructure service operators).

(c) **Shifting institutions and cultural and social norms.** This involves tackling institutional, organizational, cultural, and societal norms, attitudes, and behaviors that discriminate and disadvantage females and that contribute to gender-based violence and harassment.

While the entry points suggested are intended to provide some examples, ADB project teams should consider opportunities to raise ambition on gender equality in the design of projects, so that investments can have the most sustained impact.

(ii) **ADB project teams should pay attention to the quality of interventions in terms of their ultimate impact on women and girls.** Project design features that address gender equality and women's empowerment should avoid "tick-box" practices that do not consider their full impact on women and girls. For example, while measures could be implemented to create jobs for women and girls, these could end up being low-quality or underpaid if not planned carefully. Quotas for women and girls' involvement could be instituted, but if these do not reflect the local context, they could fail or even cause backlash. Project teams should consider all measures in terms of their impact on women and girls and be monitored effectively, ideally with the participation of women and girls affected.

(iii) **Women and girls are not a homogenous group.** In practice, not all women and girls are disadvantaged in the same way. The extent to which they may be excluded depends on intersecting identities and being from different or multiple vulnerable or marginalized groups (for example disability, age, sexuality, race or ethnicity, or socioeconomic status). While this paper refers to women and girls, it is important to take a wider view of how women and men face multiple and overlapping forms of discrimination. Project teams should identify these diverse forms of discrimination and exclusion, especially as part of the gender analysis. Spatial factors also play a role in the level of exclusion or discrimination faced by women and girls and in their access to infrastructure (for example, where in cities they are, or whether they are in urban or rural areas).

(iv) **Gender equality is not just about women and girls.** When working in sensitive environments, it is important to consider the risks of backlash and identify strategies to mitigate these risks. Gender equality is about creating opportunities for all—regardless of gender—rather than preferential treatment of women and girls. Section 2.1 for example, outlines some of how women and girls are at a specific disadvantage. A critical part of achieving gender equality and preventing backlash can include spending time upfront in building relationships and building trust in the project; working with men and boys to change discriminatory attitudes about women and girls; engaging high profile male leaders to advocate for gender equality; and referring to gender equality principles enshrined in national laws and policies.

3.2 Pathways of Change

This section provides an overview of the causal pathways that inform specific project feature examples in section 3 and underpins the theory of change diagrams in section 4. This provides an overview of what leads to positive change for gender equality and women's empowerment in the context of infrastructure projects.

Given the complexity of infrastructure sectors, it is difficult to define individual causal pathways at a high level. This report offers five approaches that represent key pathways to change. While these pathways are represented as condensed, linear pathways of change for the sake of illustration, in practice a combination of approaches is required to achieve the desired outcomes. Where possible, ADB project teams should design projects drawing on a number of these pathways:

(i) **Better physical design:** Integrating and prioritizing women's needs in infrastructure design codes, standards, and guidelines.

(ii) **Inclusive service design:** Planning service delivery and operation of infrastructure to include women's needs and priorities.

(iii) **Increase stakeholder understanding:** Supporting stakeholders to better understand and respond to women's needs and priorities through training, capacity building, and awareness raising.

(iv) **Increase women's decision-making:** Strengthening women's representation and decision-making power in infrastructure design, delivery, and operations (leading to more inclusive programs and outcomes).

(v) **Institutional change:** Shifting institutional practices, systems, and cultures to incorporate women's needs and priorities in policies and processes (leading to transformative changes).

These indicative causal pathways are intended as a road map for developing more detailed pathways and logic for diverse specific sub-themes and activities, which project teams should do at the project level. Projects should develop and own causal pathways and project specific theories of change as part of the DMF process. For specific subsectors and initiatives, the logic and assumptions need to be firmly grounded in the real-life context, experience, and institutional practice at the level of intervention.

Therefore, these overarching causal pathways can be drawn on to design effective project level theories of change and identify activities needed to achieve desired outcomes. Examples are provided that illustrate how these pathways lead to change.

(i) **Better Physical Design:** Women's needs are prioritized and embedded in infrastructure design codes, standards, and guidelines.

A primary way in which infrastructure contributes to women's safety, reduces time poverty, enhances mobility, and unlocks economic opportunities can be traced to physical design and spatial planning. Women's needs and priorities are not often reflected in design, and women are traditionally underrepresented in professions related to urban development or infrastructure (The Solutions Lab 2020). To respond to this, the theory of change incorporates several measures to embed women's needs and priorities in urban planning, design codes, standards, and guidelines. This, in turn, will influence the nature of the physical infrastructure built. For example:

- Embedding requirements for the proximity of housing, services, and transport nodes leads to urban areas that are arranged according to the journeys and needs of both women and men in all their diversity (World Bank 2020). This results in more walkable cities that reduce the need for motorized transport and improve safety for women as they move around the city (Arup 2022; World Bank 2020).
- Developing design standards that reflect women's needs by, for example, requiring a mix of layouts and typologies that support a variety of life stages and needs, leads to more buying options that suit the needs of women and men; and housing built with space for care or economic activities (UN-Habitat 2014). This results in more women being able to engage in home-based work, on which many women are dependent (F. Bonnet et al. 2021).
- Developing design guidance on safety in public spaces, transport stations and stops, and WASH facilities to require adequate lighting, sight lines, active frontage, rounded corners, and similar features, lead to spaces with natural surveillance and being more welcoming for women, including at night (Arup 2022). This results in women being able to move about more freely in a wider range of hours, accessing economic, education, and health opportunities as well as improved safety (World Bank 2020). Box 1 and Annex 2 provide further information.
- Requiring minimum standards for the design of emergency shelters—including on-site security, provisions to protect privacy, and safe and appropriate sanitary facilities— leads to the construction of shelters that meet the safety and privacy needs of women (M. H. Bhuiyan 2013). This results in a reduction of harm to women during an emergency.
- Embedding requirements for universal design standards leads to more accessible stations, transport, pavements, and footpaths that support different types of journeys (for example, in many contexts women are more likely to travel via nonmotorized transport or with passengers). This results in increased usage of infrastructure built by all citizens, including women, but also older people or people with reduced mobility.
- Embedding requirements into procurement can lead to increased incentives for suppliers to demonstrate capability and measures to respond to women's needs and priorities in the design and construction of physical infrastructure. This results in wider recognition of women as a key target demographic in the infrastructure sector.

Box 1: Case Study—The Livable Cities Investment Project for Balanced Development in Georgia

The Livable Cities Investment Project for Balanced Development in Georgia—funded by ADB—aims to improve livability and foster economic growth by creating inclusive and climate-resilient infrastructure. Key gender-related features include implementing local guidance on gender-sensitive urban infrastructure planning in the construction of public facilities, providing gender-based violence and sexual harassment awareness materials that include reporting protocols and hotlines, and supporting women-led enterprises. While project evaluations are not available as of 2023, they demonstrate the adoption of gender mainstreaming practices and pathways to create more accessible and safe urban spaces, provide access to gender-based violence and harassment services, and build institutional capacity for gender equality in infrastructure design.

Source: ADB. 2021. *Georgia: Livable Cities Investment Project for Balanced Development*. Manila.

(ii) **Inclusive Service Design:** Service delivery and operation of infrastructure is planned to include women's needs and priorities.

Beyond the physical design and location of infrastructure, the design and delivery of infrastructure-related services play a crucial role in shaping women's access and impact. Activities that seek to incorporate women's needs and concerns in the design of services enable infrastructure to better serve the wider population. For example:

- Using sex-disaggregated data and analysis—including in market analysis related to utilities—to inform and design tariff structures, fees, financial products, and business models leads to more affordable options for women—including in female-headed households and businesses—to pay for services. This results in increased access to these services for women, as well as increased revenue streams for companies and providers.
- Incorporating women's travel patterns and journeys into transport service planning—including schedules, network coverage, efficiency, and modal connections—leads to transport networks that better meet the needs and priorities of women. This results in reduced time spent on transport and enhances women's mobility and access to economic opportunities, education, and health care.
- The design of support services for gender-based violence or harassment in infrastructure settings (such as in stations or WASH facilities) leads to greater enforcement and deterrence against perpetrators. This results in women feeling safer to use services and facilities and increasing the customer base.

(iii) **Increase Stakeholder Understanding:** Stakeholders are supported to better understand and respond to women's needs and priorities through training and capacity building.

There is a gender gap when it comes to the types of training, skills, and qualifications often needed in the infrastructure sector. Providing training and capacity building to stakeholders can lead to wider adoption of gender inclusion in infrastructure projects. For example:

- Training women with the necessary qualifications or capacity building can lead them to better advocate for their needs and/or attain employment in infrastructure sectors. This results in an increased labor force participation of women, as well as enhanced performance and service delivery for utility companies or service providers.
- Training men and other stakeholders—such as technical experts and decision-makers—on the needs of women leads to increased sensitivity and capability of institutions to better respond to women's needs. This results in shifting social norms and increased prioritization of women's needs in infrastructure design and delivery, as well as helping to reduce backlash to perceived preferential treatment of women.
- Delivery of public outreach and communication campaigns on sexual violence can lead to shifts in social norms around the acceptability of key issues of concern to women related to infrastructure, such as gender-based violence and harassment. This results in women feeling safer in accessing infrastructure services and can influence men's behaviors (Arup 2022).

These approaches are a key part of delivering change around how women experience and can participate in the delivery of infrastructure and its impacts.

(iv) **Increase Women's Decision-Making:** Increasing women's representation and decision-making power in infrastructure design, delivery, and operations leads to more inclusive outcomes.

Women are traditionally underrepresented in institutions involved in the delivery of infrastructure. This includes employment, leadership, and decision-making bodies. Employing more women in utility companies, for example, not only creates direct job opportunities for more women, but evidence shows this enables institutions to better plan, design, and respond to the needs and concerns of women when delivering infrastructure. Activities designed to grow women's representation lead to more inclusive infrastructure, for example:

➔ Measures to recruit and retain women employees—including in leadership roles—lead to more diverse companies. Women are best placed to plan and design for the needs of other women. Evidence suggests that increased diversity results in several positive effects, including enhancing the financial performance of utility companies; boosting sustainable outcomes; service and product design that better reflects the needs of women as customers; and increasing the perception of safety for women passengers on transport services (Yepez 2023).

➔ Setting requirements for women's direct and meaningful representation in decision-making bodies—such as WASH committees and municipal planning boards—leads to increased women's decision-making power and proposed infrastructure being assessed from a gender perspective. This results in infrastructure that is more accessible and meets the needs of diverse groups of women (example in Box 2).

Box 2: Case Study—Women's Leadership in the Banda Golra Water Supply Scheme, Pakistan

The Banda Golra Water Supply Scheme in Pakistan aimed to address water access and sanitation challenges faced by a small village. Led by Nasim Bibi, a community-based women's organization (CBO) accessed loans from the Sarhad Rural Support Programme (SRSP) to fund the installation of seven hand pumps. Key gender-related features included tailored access to credit, women's active involvement in identifying community needs, women's leadership in managing the project, and active participation of women in project activities. The outcomes of the program included improved sanitation and health, time savings for women and girls, women's empowerment and recognition, enhanced social mobility, improved education, and increased community involvement. Key factors for success included trust and support in the community, male involvement and support, and women's financial independence. The project illustrates the multitude of benefits that arose in terms of outcomes from the meaningful involvement and leadership of women in service design and delivery.

Source: United Nations. 2006. *Gender, Water and Sanitation: Case Studies on Best Practices*.

(v) **Institutional Change:** Shifting institutions and creating incentives to better incorporate women's needs and priorities in policies and processes lead to transformative changes.

Embedding the needs and priorities of women into institutional commitments, processes, and policies is a critical way of delivering sustainable, transformative change in infrastructure. This is a vital component of sustainably enhancing gender equality and women's empowerment in the long-term, which goes beyond the limitations of capacity building, awareness raising, campaigns, and training alone in institutionalizing change. Municipal authorities, utility providers, and transport companies can be supported to adopt measures in policy and commitments on gender inclusion, providing an institutional incentive that is necessary for the measures outlined in this paper. Combined with effective transparency and accountability mechanisms, this can lead to infrastructure better reflecting and responding to the needs of women. For example:

- Requirements for master planning and metropolitan development plans to include and incorporate the needs and priorities of women lead to the spatial arrangement of urban areas aligned with how women access services and move around cities. This results in urban development which promotes women's mobility, reduces time spent on travel, and increases women's access to economic opportunities, health, and education.
- Assessment and review of disaster risk management and livelihood restoration plans to ensure they meet the distinct needs of women and men during emergencies and in post-disaster response leads to more inclusive disaster risk management during times of crisis. This results in fewer women being killed or injured during disasters and increases their ability to recover faster economically.

3.3 Entry Points and Examples

This section provides examples of project features across various entry points in infrastructure projects. These examples are not designed to be comprehensive but act as a reference for types of interventions that could be considered as part of infrastructure projects and aligned with individual project contexts. These interventions and project design features exist across a spectrum in terms of the type and extent of impact they have (section 3.1). Each set of project features in this section generally covers features at all three levels of impact, including measures to address the practical needs and priorities of women and girls; measures that support women's empowerment; and measures that could shift institutional practices and social norms. When selecting project features, consider where ambition for gender equality and women's empowerment could be raised.

Access, Pricing, and Affordability

- In demand and willingness and ability to pay studies, **collect data from both the male and female household members as well as male and female-headed households, and women-owned enterprises.**
- **Design financing solutions that reflect end users' ability to pay,** making investments in energy assets and energy efficiency more achievable and equitable for different groups (World Bank 2020; ADB 2022a).

- **Design tariffs that are affordable and flexible** to enable women to buy and use mobile phones, fridges, and other time-saving technologies that require energy, increasing productivity of home-based work and enabling time savings (Orlando et al. 2018).
- **Design measures to subsidize initial grid connection charges** for women-owned businesses, low-income and female-headed households, and poor households that cannot necessarily afford the initial large outlay such as through discounts, or the option to pay in installments (Orlando et al. 2018).
- **Partner with local finance institutions to increase access to finance for women**, developing financing instruments, mechanisms, and specific loan products that are affordable and tailored to women, including microfinance and mobile banking (ADB 2013b; UN 2018; IFC 2020). This leads to **expanded financial products for women** that can be used to pay for utilities, services, or housing.
- **Identify alternative, accessible, and affordable land-finance mechanisms** such as community savings groups. These financing mechanisms can provide women with credit quickly in times of crisis, or startup loans for income-generating activities (ADB 2013b; World Bank 2020).
- **Offer community-based savings and loan programs** that enable access to small loans for incremental housing improvements including for low income and female-headed households (ADB 2013b; World Bank 2020).
- **Collaborate with community-based savings and loan schemes** to act as "brokers" for channeling loans to poor communities, providing governments and lending institutions with a proven, effective management mechanism whereby communities manage loan disbursal and repayments as a group (ADB 2013b; World Bank 2020).

Urban Planning Guidelines

- **Assess urban spaces through a safety lens.** Incorporate design features such as gradual gradients, rounded corners, and natural lighting to enhance sightlines (improving visual awareness); calming artwork and soundscapes ease feelings of threat and promote high footfall that generates natural surveillance. These features have been shown to enhance perceptions of safety for women (ADB 2013b; Arup 2022).
- **Implement measures to slow vehicular traffic and improve pedestrian infrastructure,** including sidewalks that are sufficiently wide, well paved, and free from parked cars; reduced vehicular lanes; raised crosswalks; and increased cycle lane and public transport lane widths. Given that women tend to be more reliant on nonmotorized transport, the incorporation of such features in road design can lead to **streets that are safer and more accessible for women** as well as men (ADB 2013a; World Bank 2020).
- **Develop plans that combine public spaces with key public and social services** and incorporate requirements on adequate public lighting to increase visibility at night, particularly around bus stops, active streetscapes, and spaces that are safer for women (ADB 2013b; World Bank 2020).
- **Improve lighting design in streets and public spaces,** including the use of night-time vulnerability assessments to identify lighting requirements that lead to urban spaces that have improved perceptions of safety (Arup 2022; ADB 2013a).
- **Use digital technology and apps to raise awareness and share knowledge about public safety.** Develop campaigns or utilize specialist apps to raise awareness of women's safety in urban areas, while providing a support mechanism for reporting (ADB 2015b; ADB 2022b; Arup 2022).

- **Support municipalities to undertake a gender-based assessment of budgets to understand the differentiated impact on women and men and low-income households**, integrating a gender perspective throughout all stages of the budgeting process, and restructuring revenues and expenditures to promote gender equality, including in partnership with key women's groups and civil society (Council of Europe 2009; OECD 2023; UN-Women 2018).
- **Embed requirements into planning policy for adequate context-specific infrastructure and services** close to housing (for example from 250 meters to 500 meters walking distance). Project teams should determine and test with residents to ensure services are conveniently located. This results in neighborhoods that better support the diverse mobility needs and responsibilities of girls, women, and men (e.g., economic activities and care) (World Bank 2020).

Transport Planning

- **Collect sex-disaggregated transport and travel pattern data,** including trip purpose by mode, journeys taken, by whom, to where, alongside a baseline (ADB 2013a). This data should also be disaggregated by age and disability.
- **Develop bus and train schedules that consider the different needs of women and men** and diverse travel patterns beyond traditional commuting patterns to allow for trip chaining and last-mile connections (ADB 2013a; World Bank 2020).
- **Improve the frequency and reliability of transit services**—especially during nonpeak hours and at night—to reduce waiting times and provide convenient, safe service outside traditional commuting hours that enable women's mobility outside busy times. Enhance lighting, natural surveillance, and visibility at stops through design to enhance women's safety (Arup 2022; World Bank 2020).
- **Promote the use of innovative technology platforms, apps, and data** to enhance women's safety. For example, apps such as the OpenSidewalks Project in the United States help pedestrians plan journeys, reducing time spent walking alone, which can be disproportionately dangerous for women (Taskar Center for Accessible Technology, n.d.). "Circle of 6" is a phone app used in Delhi that supports targets or potential targets of sexual harassment to reach out to someone they can trust to help them in a time of need and connects users to a 24-hour women's hotline (ADB 2015b).
- **Install emergency communication systems**—such as emergency call buttons or intercom systems on buses and at transit stations—which can help women quickly seek assistance in case of emergencies or incidents. London, United Kingdom, has implemented the "Help Point" system on their public transport network, allowing passengers to contact staff directly.
- **Provide flexible, affordable, and accessible multimodal transportation options** that cater to gendered transport behaviors, such as trip-chaining, and reliance on walking or public transport (ADB 2013a; World Bank 2020).
- **Implement fare structures for public transport that include flexible options**—such as unlimited rides—and do not disproportionately burden those who tend to make multiple short trips with transfers, such as primary caregivers. Test pricing for affordability based on average household expenditures (ADB 2013a; ICED 2017; World Bank 2020).
- **Design transportation infrastructure with considerations for different age groups, abilities, body sizes, and needs**, including lower step-ups, appropriate handrails, and dedicated storage spaces, enhancing access for all passengers (ADB 2013a; World Bank 2020).

- **Establish clean and secure toilet facilities with diaper-changing spaces (in both male and female facilities)** within or within a short walking distance of bus stops and stations (ADB 2013a; World Bank 2020).
- **Create job opportunities for women in transportation through infrastructure investments** and promote their economic participation, including by promoting the role of women in perceived male-dominated jobs; supporting women contractors to bid for transport construction contracts, hiring women ticket collectors and drivers as well as female engineers and technical specialists; and allocation of shop spaces at stations for women's businesses (ADB 2013a; ICED 2017).
- **Ensure female representation on transport planning committees** and involve women's groups in participatory analysis of gender barriers and solutions (ICED 2017).
- **Implement communications to drive behavior change** (e.g., posters, apps, advertising campaigns, or social media campaigns) empowering all to act and discourage sexual harassment (ADB 2015b).
- **Support women entrepreneurs in scaling up sustainable transport innovations** through accelerators and inclusive procurement strategies (Biegel and Lambin 2021).
- **Provide training on the impact of violence against women and harassment to transport operators**, enforcing zero-tolerance policies within transport agencies backed up by systems and processes for reporting and responding to incidents (ADB 2015b; ICED 2017).
- **Support public sector transportation authorities to understand and address the transport needs of both women and men in transport planning.** This could include involving staff in activities to increase awareness of different needs, incorporating gender considerations into guidelines, and establishing structured interactions with women's organizations (ICED 2017) (Box 3).

Box 3: Case Study—GreenCell Electric Bus Financing Project

The GreenCell Electric Bus Financing Project in India—funded by the Asian Development Bank (ADB) and implemented by GreenCell Mobility Private Limited (GMPL)—aims to improve public transport options while prioritizing gender equality and women's empowerment. India recognizes the need to transition to alternative means of transport and increase public transport usage to address urbanization challenges and reduce greenhouse gas emissions. The project incorporates gender-responsive measures into privately operated bus transportation, focusing on enhancing safety and security features and providing leadership training for women staff. Key gender-related project features include conducting a women's safety audit, installing women-friendly safety features in vehicles and bus depots, providing safety response protocol training, implementing a women's leadership program, recruiting female interns for technical positions, and raising awareness on gender inclusive initiatives. The project outputs include expanding the operation of green and safer-for-women transportation systems, generating local employment opportunities, and enhancing gender equality in employment opportunities and working conditions at GMPL.

Source: ADB. 2022c. *India: GreenCell Electric Bus Financing Project*.

Design Specifications and Guidance for Housing and Shelter

- **Establish minimum standards for accessible and inclusive design**, such as formalized divisions of space and in-home water and sanitation facilities (Reall 2021). This leads to housing developments that support a variety of women's and men's needs.
- **Develop plans for diverse housing typologies** to ensure people with different lifestyle needs, household arrangements, and financial capacities have equitable access to quality housing (World Bank 2020). This leads to **housing developments that better reflect the diverse roles women and men play in cities**.
- **Encourage mixed-use zoning and design houses that allow for economic activities within the dwelling,** increasing income-generating opportunities within residential units. For example, 40% of floor space is dedicated to economic use within any given neighborhood area. (World Bank 2020). Measures such as this would lead to **housing that supports women's potential for home-based entrepreneurship.**
- **Incorporate women's safety features in shelter design guidelines and standards** including adequate lighting, on-site security, provisions to protect privacy, and safe and appropriate sanitary facilities (UNHCR 2008; UN-Habitat 2014; Erman et al. 2021).

Housing, Tenure, and Land

- **Provide a variety of tenure types in housing developments** including customary types of tenure, joint titles for women and men, leaseholds, condominiums, cooperatives, shared leaseholds, and diverse rental options (World Bank 2020).
- **Incorporate gender-informed allocation criteria for housing developments** based on a baseline of local disadvantaged populations. For example, a percentage allocation of affordable housing for disadvantaged groups (low-income households, single parents, older people, and youth) of which a crosscutting percentage is allocated to vulnerable women or men (UN-Habitat 2014).
- **Provide training, information, and legal support for women on land rights** to address gaps, unclear provisions, and discriminatory laws (UN-Habitat 2014). Supporting women with paralegal training on land rights can help women to successfully obtain landownership and certificates of tenure, shift local institutions to become more understanding of land problems, and support women to become trusted advisors and experts on land and property rights (Arup 2022).
- **Support women's land action trusts.** These can be an important mechanism to support poorer urban women to access land and housing as well as financial advice and support. **These trusts can facilitate engagement between communities and decision-makers** (Arup 2022).
- **Engage women and girls in creating land tenure policies.** Engage women, particularly female heads of households, on urban land governance, security of tenure policies, and in dialogue on land-tenure regularization (ADB 2013b; Arup 2022).
- **Incorporate joint titling into housing development or resettlement activities.** This includes where both women and men are on housing titles or female-headed households (ADB 2013b; UN-Habitat 2012; UN-Habitat 2014; World Bank 2020).

Women's Representation, Decision-Making Roles, and Leadership

- **Implement participatory research and data collection processes** to attain more accurate qualitative and quantitative sex-disaggregated data and to understand social and gender norms, attitudes, and behaviors (ADB 2013b; World Bank 2020).
- **Hire resident leaders—including women—to help mobilize the wider community** to be involved in the planning and design process. Establish goals for participation that mirror the gender composition of the community. For instance, if the community consists of 60% females, aim for a participant group that similarly comprises 60% females (World Bank 2020).
- **Hire women of different ages and abilities—where appropriate—to facilitate participatory planning and design processes and activities** including ensuring robust facilitation measures to gain input from women and minorities during meetings, data collection, or other engagement activities (World Bank 2020).
- **Enhance the capabilities of organizations dedicated to women-centric business models,** empowering them to cultivate technical, business, leadership, and advocacy proficiencies. Prioritize the advancement of women into leadership positions across all levels. (ADB 2013b; UN 2018).
- **Build in formal roles for women in decision-making structures through such mechanisms as quotas in local government or user associations, WASH program staff, and WASH committees**, and accompany this with training, oversight, targeted support for women to assume leadership positions, promoting active participation (ADB 2013b; Das, M.B. 2017; World Bank 2020).

Enhancing Women's Employment in Municipal Authorities, Utility, and Transport Companies

- **Design and implement human resource policies** that incentivize hiring and retaining women (Das 2017; USAID 2023).
- **Consider project targets and incentives** to encourage women's employment at all levels (ADB 2022a; Orlando et al. 2018; USAID 2023).
- **Employ women in energy service provision** including sales, meter reading, billing, awareness-raising, and payment collection to build trust and expand reach into underserved communities (ADB 2022a; World Bank 2020).
- **Introduce measures for work environments that appeal to women as well as men** including introducing flexible working policies, work-life balance, safer working conditions, paid parental/maternity/paternity leave, on-site childcare facilities, and a clear diversity, equity, and inclusion policy (ADB 2022a; Orlando et al. 2018). This creates incentives to attract and retain women employees as well as improving working conditions for all employees.
- **Support women's career progression** including identifying women leaders to showcase the role of women in the sector; building leadership and managerial capacity of women at all levels; and offering mentorship programs to female as well as male staff (Das 2017).
- **Complement institutional policies, systems, processes, and incentives that support women's progression and that reward positive behaviors with internal outreach and communications on cultural biases and stereotypes around women's work in male-dominated infrastructure companies** including efforts to educate and inform staff about the value and capabilities of women in technical roles. This helps to build a corporate culture that supports and empowers women (ADB 2022a; USAID 2023).

Box 4: Case Study—Promoting Women's Employment in District Heating Projects, Kazakhstan

This European Bank for Reconstruction and Development (EBRD) funded project aimed to improve the efficiency of heating systems while addressing gender imbalances in the sector. Gender assessments conducted in three cities revealed that the majority of employees in district heating companies were men, particularly in technical positions. Women were primarily employed in administrative roles. To address this, the company prioritized female technical students for internships and covered the study fees of seven students, four of whom were female. In Aktau, a gender-sensitive employment strategy was implemented to address customer preferences. Women were employed to visit households for meter readings and utility payment collection. These initiatives led to improved customer service, operational efficiency, and the recognition of women as key customers. Additionally, supporting women's education and employment in science, technology, engineering, and mathematics (STEM) fields contributed to a more diverse workforce, meeting the practical and strategic needs of the company, its employees, and its customers.

Sources: European Bank for Reconstruction and Development. 2014. *Gender Assessment of District Heating Projects in Kazakhstan financed by the Clean Technology Fund* (CTF). European Bank for Reconstruction and Development (EBRD) and Climate Investment Funds (CIF). 2016. *Gender Mainstreaming in District Heating Projects in the Commonwealth of Independent States: A Toolkit.*

Reflecting the Needs and Priorities of Women in Climate Resilience

Disaster risk management and livelihood restoration plans reviewed for gender inclusion, for example:

- **Ensure mitigation and preparedness phases of disaster management assess and plan for differentiated impacts on diverse groups of girls and women** to enable long-term and development-oriented recovery actions (World Bank 2020).
- **Develop culturally appropriate early warning systems** with education and awareness programs to explicitly target women of all ages and abilities, including in diverse cultural groups and hazard contexts. These measures will result in early warning systems being delivered which reach more women (Erman et al. 2021).
- **Channel funding through microfinance institutions and community-based savings** and loan schemes to provide low-interest credit that will strengthen the capabilities of women to prepare for and recover economically from disaster (World Bank 2020).
- **When establishing priorities for new housing assignments, direct attention toward extremely vulnerable women** including single mothers, widows, women with low income or without employment, socially marginalized women, and others recognized at the local level through the insights of knowledgeable women in the community (UN-Habitat 2014)
- **Deliver community sensitization on evacuation plans** ensuring that women as well as men provide and receive community planning and outreach (Erman et al. 2021)(Box 5 provides an example).
- **Integrate women's economic empowerment measures in recovery** frameworks, sector-based recovery plans, and monitoring and evaluation frameworks for equitable resource allocation and needs prioritization during recovery (World Bank 2020). This should include women's participation in the design, implementation, and monitoring of response and recovery programs.

Box 5: Case Study—Community-Based Flood Management Program in Bangladesh

The project aimed to reduce the vulnerability of people, particularly women, to floods and enhance the capacity of high-risk communities to mitigate emergencies. Gender-related features of the program included the inclusion of sex-disaggregated data, setting recruitment quotas for female volunteers, providing gender-specific training and livelihood support, and involving local leaders to address cultural and religious constraints. The impact of the program was evident in the timely and effective response to floods and lower flood impact in the program areas. The recruitment of more women as volunteers and into leadership roles contributed to increased access, improved quality of life, enhanced disaster preparedness, and better hygiene standards for women and their families. The involvement of local leaders was crucial in facilitating women's participation and program implementation.

Source: International Federation of Red Cross and Red Crescent Societies. 2010. *A Practical Guide to Gender-sensitive Approaches for Disaster Management*.

⊙ **Integrate the reduction of gender-based violence into disaster risk management policies and plans** at all stages, including preparedness, post-disaster response, and recovery (World Bank 2020).

Training, Capacity Building, and Communications on Women's Needs and Priorities

⊙ **Conduct training to enhance women's knowledge and skills** in contributing to service design processes. Establish policies and procedures to support women's career progression and opportunities to take up senior management and decision-making roles.

⊙ **Establish funding streams and scholarships for higher education programs for women** in science, technology, engineering, and mathematics (STEM)-related subjects, including civil and water engineering, water resources management, and environmental science (World Bank 2020).

⊙ **Design and provide vocational training in vulnerable communities targeting women**. This was found to lead to **energy projects that better incorporated gender considerations**, and it can be effective in **reducing gender gaps in skills and access to jobs** (Orlando et al. 2018).

⊙ **Train women in traditionally male-dominated technical professions** such as carpentry, masonry, construction, and mechanical engineering areas (ADB 2013b). Training design should consider domestic, regional, or international skills accreditation and recognized standards.

⊙ **Develop capacity building workshops for staff and senior management within municipal authorities** to be trained by local women's organizations to better understand the safety concerns, business case, and differentiated needs of women (ADB 2013; ADB 2015b; ADB 2018; UN-Habitat 2012).

⊙ **Require comprehensive gender training, balanced job quotas, and the creation of gender specialist teams in water and sewerage or other utility service providers**, with specific emphasis on enhancing competence and awareness within departments responsible for informal settlements. (World Bank 2020).

4 SECTOR THEORIES OF CHANGE

This section provides theories of change for how infrastructure projects can achieve outcomes on gender equality through the integration of gender related features. It is designed to align with the ADB design and monitoring framework (DMF) development process and facilitate the selection of outcome indicators by illustrating the activities involved, outputs, and causal pathways. Given the breadth of the infrastructure sector and the magnitude of subsectors it includes, separate theories of change (TOCs) have been developed for the **Urban Development (Figure 1), Transport (Figure 2), WASH (Figure 3),** and **Energy (Figure 4)** sectors. These TOCs intend to support ADB colleagues and partners designing projects in relevant sectors to identify project activities, outputs, and outcomes for gender equality.

Structure of the Theories of Change

- The starting point is a series of **problem statements**, which illustrate how women are disproportionately affected by a lack of access to suitable infrastructure.
- **Outcomes** were selected to reflect and respond to these key challenges, and a collection of **outputs** was identified to achieve these outcomes.
- Examples of **activities** are provided that are needed to deliver these outputs. These draw from the entry points outlined in section 2.
- **Assumptions and risks** are provided for each sector.
- **Common causal pathways** are based on those presented in section 3.2.

Using These Theories of Change

- **The TOCs are not designed to be comprehensive.** Given the expansive number of topics that fall under infrastructure investment, it was not possible to develop comprehensive theories of change for each sector, nor was it possible to go into a high level of detail. Instead, these diagrams are intended to illustrate key higher level project features and examples that could apply to a broad range of projects. This section seeks to highlight common causal pathways that can be adapted at the project level for different infrastructure investments (section 4.5).
- **The TOCs focus only on gender-related features of infrastructure projects.** The tables feature only outcomes, outputs, and activities related to gender equality. In practice, results chains will have to integrate these features either alongside other activities, outputs, and outcomes, or consider how the nature of intended outcomes, outputs, and activities could be altered to address women's needs and priorities in the ways described in this report.

◉ **The TOCs feature activities, outputs, and outcomes across a range of impact levels.** Building on the impact levels presented in section 3.1.1, the TOCs reflect a variety of interventions including those that address the needs and priorities of women and girls; measures that support women's empowerment, including in economic activities and representation; and measures that support institutional change or shifting social and cultural norms (such as the incorporation of gender considerations into institutional policies and guidelines).

◉ **The categorization of activities and outputs may vary depending on the project.** Supporting policy and measures to incorporate gender inclusion can be considered as a prerequisite or activity before the delivery of the infrastructure. In some projects, however, inclusive measures or policies could be considered an output. ADB project teams should consider this on a project-by-project basis when designing the results chain.

Beyond boundaries. A glimpse into the varied roles women play across different sectors, adding depth to the infrastructure narrative (photos by ADB).

➔ **The TOCs are designed to align with the ADB DMF Guidelines.** This means that the diagrams focus on the results chain as defined in the DMF. As a result, impact level is not included, as this is normally determined according to in-country policies or frameworks from developing member countries. Furthermore, as the TOCs are focused on the results chain, inputs are also not included.

➔ **An extensive list of assumptions and risks is provided.** However, some assumptions and risks may not be relevant in a particular context. Programs need to conduct a thorough gender analysis to provide evidence of possible assumptions and risks and a shorter list to be agreed upon before implementation.

➔ **Corresponding indicators at output and outcome levels are provided in Annex 1.** For the outputs and outcomes presented in these diagrams, a menu of corresponding example indicators has been provided. This is to provide insight into the selection of appropriate indicators, which needs to be decided on a project-by-project basis.

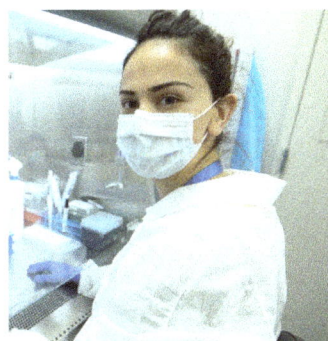

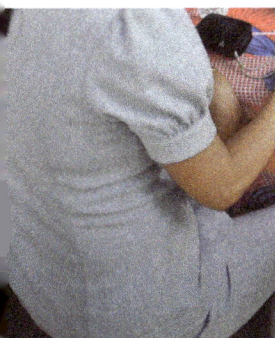

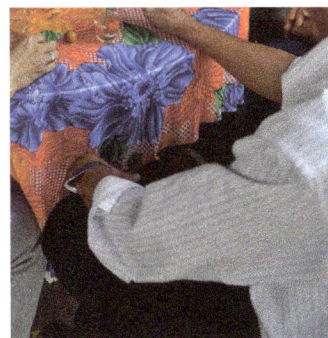

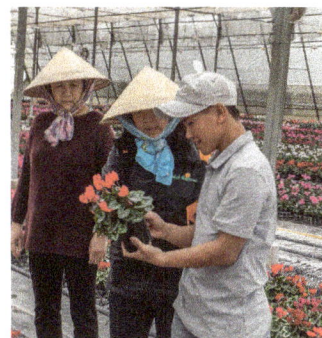

4.1. Urban Development Sector Theory of Change (Figure 1)

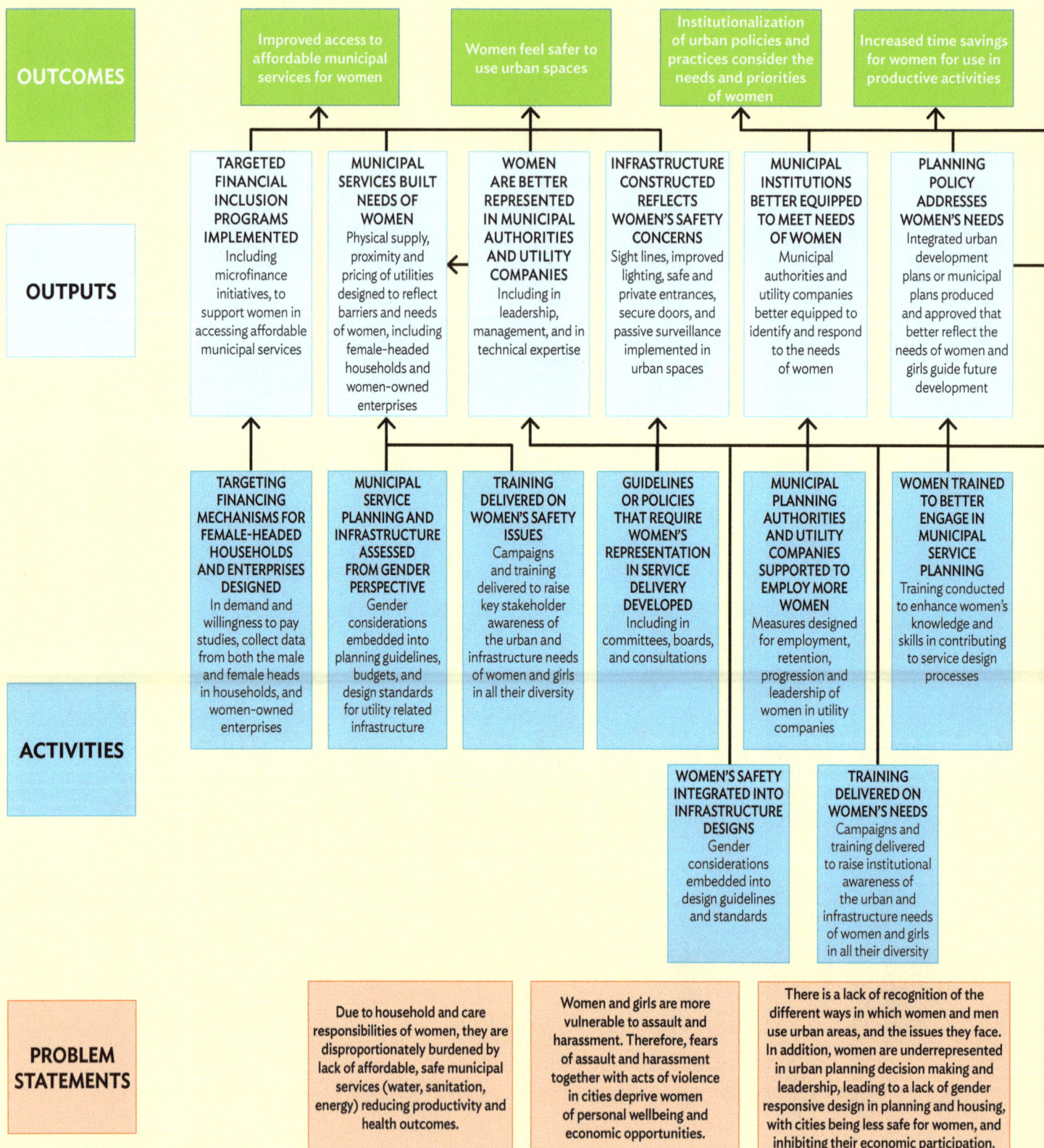

OUTCOMES

- Improved access to affordable municipal services for women
- Women feel safer to use urban spaces
- Institutionalization of urban policies and practices consider the needs and priorities of women
- Increased time savings for women for use in productive activities

OUTPUTS

TARGETED FINANCIAL INCLUSION PROGRAMS IMPLEMENTED
Including microfinance initiatives, to support women in accessing affordable municipal services

MUNICIPAL SERVICES BUILT NEEDS OF WOMEN
Physical supply, proximity and pricing of utilities designed to reflect barriers and needs of women, including female-headed households and women-owned enterprises

WOMEN ARE BETTER REPRESENTED IN MUNICIPAL AUTHORITIES AND UTILITY COMPANIES
Including in leadership, management, and in technical expertise

INFRASTRUCTURE CONSTRUCTED REFLECTS WOMEN'S SAFETY CONCERNS
Sight lines, improved lighting, safe and private entrances, secure doors, and passive surveillance implemented in urban spaces

MUNICIPAL INSTITUTIONS BETTER EQUIPPED TO MEET NEEDS OF WOMEN
Municipal authorities and utility companies better equipped to identify and respond to the needs of women

PLANNING POLICY ADDRESSES WOMEN'S NEEDS
Integrated urban development plans or municipal plans produced and approved that better reflect the needs of women and girls guide future development

ACTIVITIES

TARGETING FINANCING MECHANISMS FOR FEMALE-HEADED HOUSEHOLDS AND ENTERPRISES DESIGNED
In demand and willingness to pay studies, collect data from both the male and female heads in households, and women-owned enterprises

MUNICIPAL SERVICE PLANNING AND INFRASTRUCTURE ASSESSED FROM GENDER PERSPECTIVE
Gender considerations embedded into planning guidelines, budgets, and design standards for utility related infrastructure

TRAINING DELIVERED ON WOMEN'S SAFETY ISSUES
Campaigns and training delivered to raise key stakeholder awareness of the urban and infrastructure needs of women and girls in all their diversity

GUIDELINES OR POLICIES THAT REQUIRE WOMEN'S REPRESENTATION IN SERVICE DELIVERY DEVELOPED
Including in committees, boards, and consultations

MUNICIPAL PLANNING AUTHORITIES AND UTILITY COMPANIES SUPPORTED TO EMPLOY MORE WOMEN
Measures designed for employment, retention, progression and leadership of women in utility companies

WOMEN TRAINED TO BETTER ENGAGE IN MUNICIPAL SERVICE PLANNING
Training conducted to enhance women's knowledge and skills in contributing to service design processes

WOMEN'S SAFETY INTEGRATED INTO INFRASTRUCTURE DESIGNS
Gender considerations embedded into design guidelines and standards

TRAINING DELIVERED ON WOMEN'S NEEDS
Campaigns and training delivered to raise institutional awareness of the urban and infrastructure needs of women and girls in all their diversity

PROBLEM STATEMENTS

Due to household and care responsibilities of women, they are disproportionately burdened by lack of affordable, safe municipal services (water, sanitation, energy) reducing productivity and health outcomes.

Women and girls are more vulnerable to assault and harassment. Therefore, fears of assault and harassment together with acts of violence in cities deprive women of personal wellbeing and economic opportunities.

There is a lack of recognition of the different ways in which women and men use urban areas, and the issues they face. In addition, women are underrepresented in urban planning decision making and leadership, leading to a lack of gender responsive design in planning and housing, with cities being less safe for women, and inhibiting their economic participation.

Source: Compiled by authors.

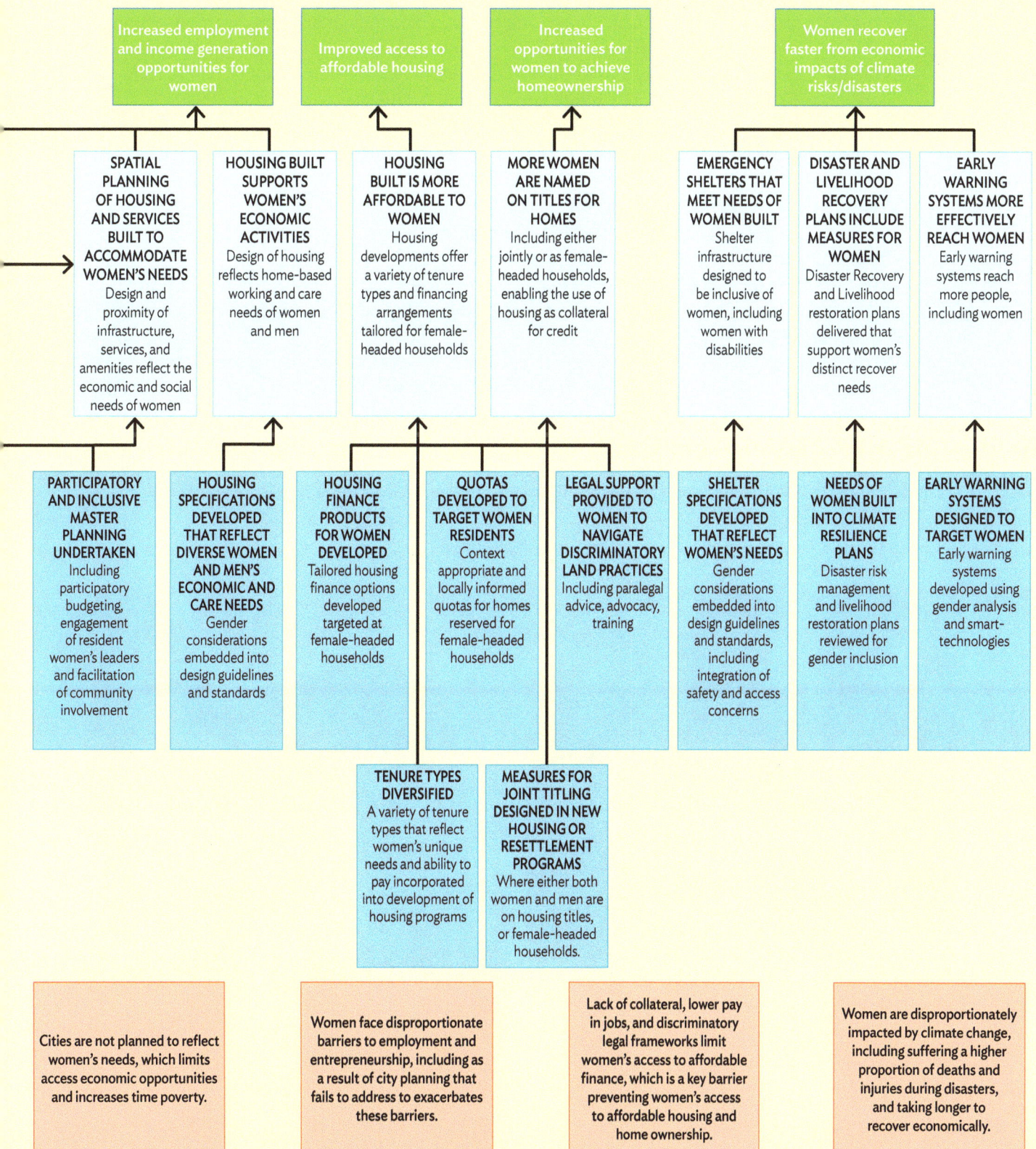

Outcomes (green)

Increased employment and income generation opportunities for women

Improved access to affordable housing

Increased opportunities for women to achieve homeownership

Women recover faster from economic impacts of climate risks/disasters

Intermediate outcomes (white)

SPATIAL PLANNING OF HOUSING AND SERVICES BUILT TO ACCOMMODATE WOMEN'S NEEDS
Design and proximity of infrastructure, services, and amenities reflect the economic and social needs of women

HOUSING BUILT SUPPORTS WOMEN'S ECONOMIC ACTIVITIES
Design of housing reflects home-based working and care needs of women and men

HOUSING BUILT IS MORE AFFORDABLE TO WOMEN
Housing developments offer a variety of tenure types and financing arrangements tailored for female-headed households

MORE WOMEN ARE NAMED ON TITLES FOR HOMES
Including either jointly or as female-headed households, enabling the use of housing as collateral for credit

EMERGENCY SHELTERS THAT MEET NEEDS OF WOMEN BUILT
Shelter infrastructure designed to be inclusive of women, including women with disabilities

DISASTER AND LIVELIHOOD RECOVERY PLANS INCLUDE MEASURES FOR WOMEN
Disaster Recovery and Livelihood restoration plans delivered that support women's distinct recover needs

EARLY WARNING SYSTEMS MORE EFFECTIVELY REACH WOMEN
Early warning systems reach more people, including women

Outputs (blue)

PARTICIPATORY AND INCLUSIVE MASTER PLANNING UNDERTAKEN
Including participatory budgeting, engagement of resident women's leaders and facilitation of community involvement

HOUSING SPECIFICATIONS DEVELOPED THAT REFLECT DIVERSE WOMEN AND MEN'S ECONOMIC AND CARE NEEDS
Gender considerations embedded into design guidelines and standards

HOUSING FINANCE PRODUCTS FOR WOMEN DEVELOPED
Tailored housing finance options developed targeted at female-headed households

QUOTAS DEVELOPED TO TARGET WOMEN RESIDENTS
Context appropriate and locally informed quotas for homes reserved for female-headed households

LEGAL SUPPORT PROVIDED TO WOMEN TO NAVIGATE DISCRIMINATORY LAND PRACTICES
Including paralegal advice, advocacy, training

SHELTER SPECIFICATIONS DEVELOPED THAT REFLECT WOMEN'S NEEDS
Gender considerations embedded into design guidelines and standards, including integration of safety and access concerns

NEEDS OF WOMEN BUILT INTO CLIMATE RESILIENCE PLANS
Disaster risk management and livelihood restoration plans reviewed for gender inclusion

EARLY WARNING SYSTEMS DESIGNED TO TARGET WOMEN
Early warning systems developed using gender analysis and smart-technologies

TENURE TYPES DIVERSIFIED
A variety of tenure types that reflect women's unique needs and ability to pay incorporated into development of housing programs

MEASURES FOR JOINT TITLING DESIGNED IN NEW HOUSING OR RESETTLEMENT PROGRAMS
Where either both women and men are on housing titles, or female-headed households.

Problem statements (orange)

Cities are not planned to reflect women's needs, which limits access economic opportunities and increases time poverty.

Women face disproportionate barriers to employment and entrepreneurship, including as a result of city planning that fails to address to exacerbates these barriers.

Lack of collateral, lower pay in jobs, and discriminatory legal frameworks limit women's access to affordable finance, which is a key barrier preventing women's access to affordable housing and home ownership.

Women are disproportionately impacted by climate change, including suffering a higher proportion of deaths and injuries during disasters, and taking longer to recover economically.

Assumptions

- Women are meaningfully involved in planning and design which leads to improvements in access and safety for all groups of women, including adolescent girls, elderly women, women with disabilities, low income groups, women entrepreneurs, and women-headed households. Similarly, gender analyses incorporate the views of women in all their diversity, where they are given the space and possibility to research and articulate the female perspective.
- Policies, plans, and regulations that consider the specific needs and priorities of women in urban spaces are implemented and enforced, with sanctions for noncompliance.
- Municipal planning authorities and transport companies have the time, interest, and budget to address women's needs and priorities.
- Initiatives to increase women's ownership of assets are matched by supporting regulations and a long-term strategy to address social norms.
- Urban planners have access to disaggregated data so they are aware of women's economic and care needs, and incorporate these needs into housing guidelines and standards, and climate-resilient plans.
- Women have access to digital devices with sufficient network coverage and are digitally literate enough to make choices that are best tailored to their transport needs and priorities, as well as to receive information on safety issues for women and in the case of emergencies.
- Transport infrastructure such as lighting, secure doors, WASH facilities, and surveillance, are adequately maintained and functioning.
- Changes to tenure types and different financing options result in increased affordability of housing for women

Empowering cities. A glimpse into women leading the charge in urban development—fostering affordable housing, shaping dynamic urban spaces, and driving inclusive and resilient economic growth (photos by ADB).

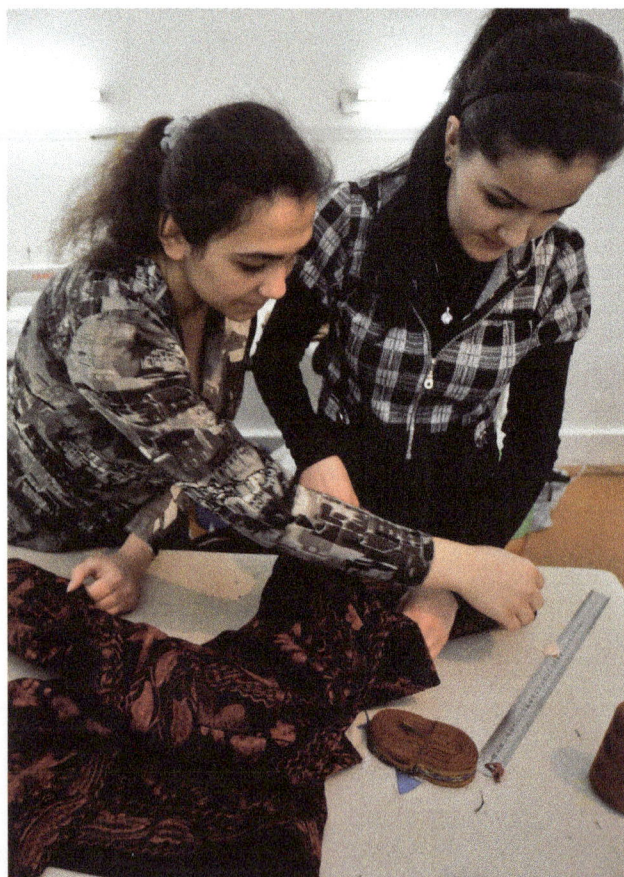

Risks

- Women employed in utility companies experience workplace discrimination and harassment, and/or there is a lack of supportive facilities and flexible working hours to balance paid work responsibilities with unpaid care, leading to poor retention and slow career progression.
- Training workshops on women's safety issues are poorly attended by travel operators and do not lead to changes in behavior.
- Decision-makers treat gender action plans and gender designs as "additional" elements and not as an integral part of the project, which may result in delays or non-implementation of gender features.

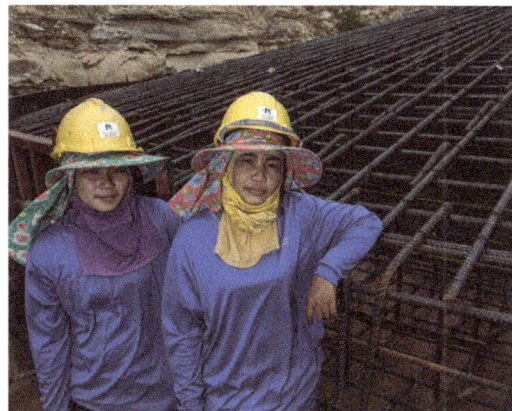

4.2. Transport Sector Theory of Change (Figure 2)

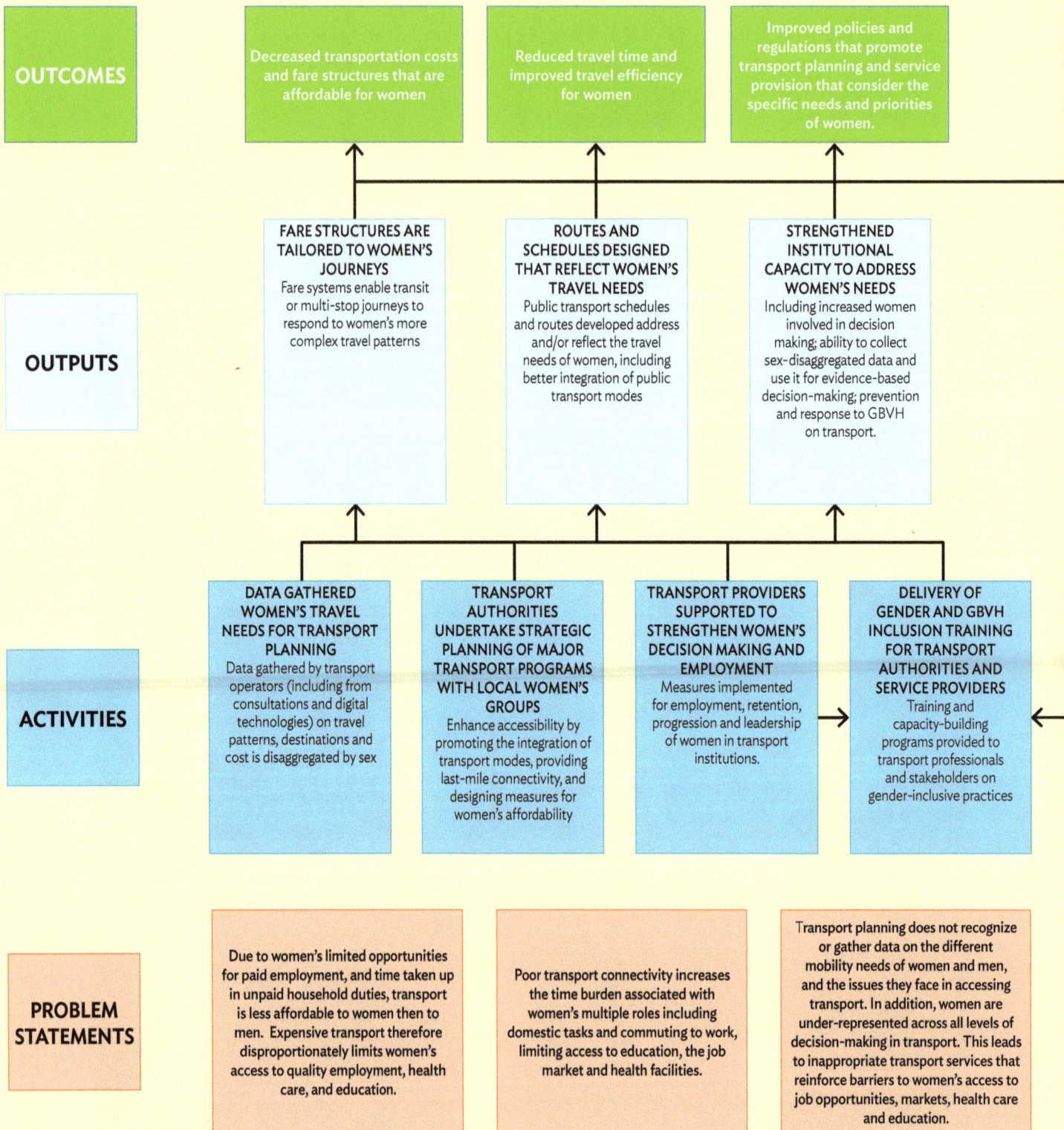

OUTCOMES

| Decreased transportation costs and fare structures that are affordable for women | Reduced travel time and improved travel efficiency for women | Improved policies and regulations that promote transport planning and service provision that consider the specific needs and priorities of women. |

OUTPUTS

FARE STRUCTURES ARE TAILORED TO WOMEN'S JOURNEYS
Fare systems enable transit or multi-stop journeys to respond to women's more complex travel patterns

ROUTES AND SCHEDULES DESIGNED THAT REFLECT WOMEN'S TRAVEL NEEDS
Public transport schedules and routes developed address and/or reflect the travel needs of women, including better integration of public transport modes

STRENGTHENED INSTITUTIONAL CAPACITY TO ADDRESS WOMEN'S NEEDS
Including increased women involved in decision making; ability to collect sex-disaggregated data and use it for evidence-based decision-making; prevention and response to GBVH on transport.

ACTIVITIES

DATA GATHERED WOMEN'S TRAVEL NEEDS FOR TRANSPORT PLANNING
Data gathered by transport operators (including from consultations and digital technologies) on travel patterns, destinations and cost is disaggregated by sex

TRANSPORT AUTHORITIES UNDERTAKE STRATEGIC PLANNING OF MAJOR TRANSPORT PROGRAMS WITH LOCAL WOMEN'S GROUPS
Enhance accessibility by promoting the integration of transport modes, providing last-mile connectivity, and designing measures for women's affordability

TRANSPORT PROVIDERS SUPPORTED TO STRENGTHEN WOMEN'S DECISION MAKING AND EMPLOYMENT
Measures implemented for employment, retention, progression and leadership of women in transport institutions.

DELIVERY OF GENDER AND GBVH INCLUSION TRAINING FOR TRANSPORT AUTHORITIES AND SERVICE PROVIDERS
Training and capacity-building programs provided to transport professionals and stakeholders on gender-inclusive practices

PROBLEM STATEMENTS

Due to women's limited opportunities for paid employment, and time taken up in unpaid household duties, transport is less affordable to women then to men. Expensive transport therefore disproportionately limits women's access to quality employment, health care, and education.

Poor transport connectivity increases the time burden associated with women's multiple roles including domestic tasks and commuting to work, limiting access to education, the job market and health facilities.

Transport planning does not recognize or gather data on the different mobility needs of women and men, and the issues they face in accessing transport. In addition, women are under-represented across all levels of decision-making in transport. This leads to inappropriate transport services that reinforce barriers to women's access to job opportunities, markets, health care and education.

Source: Compiled by authors.

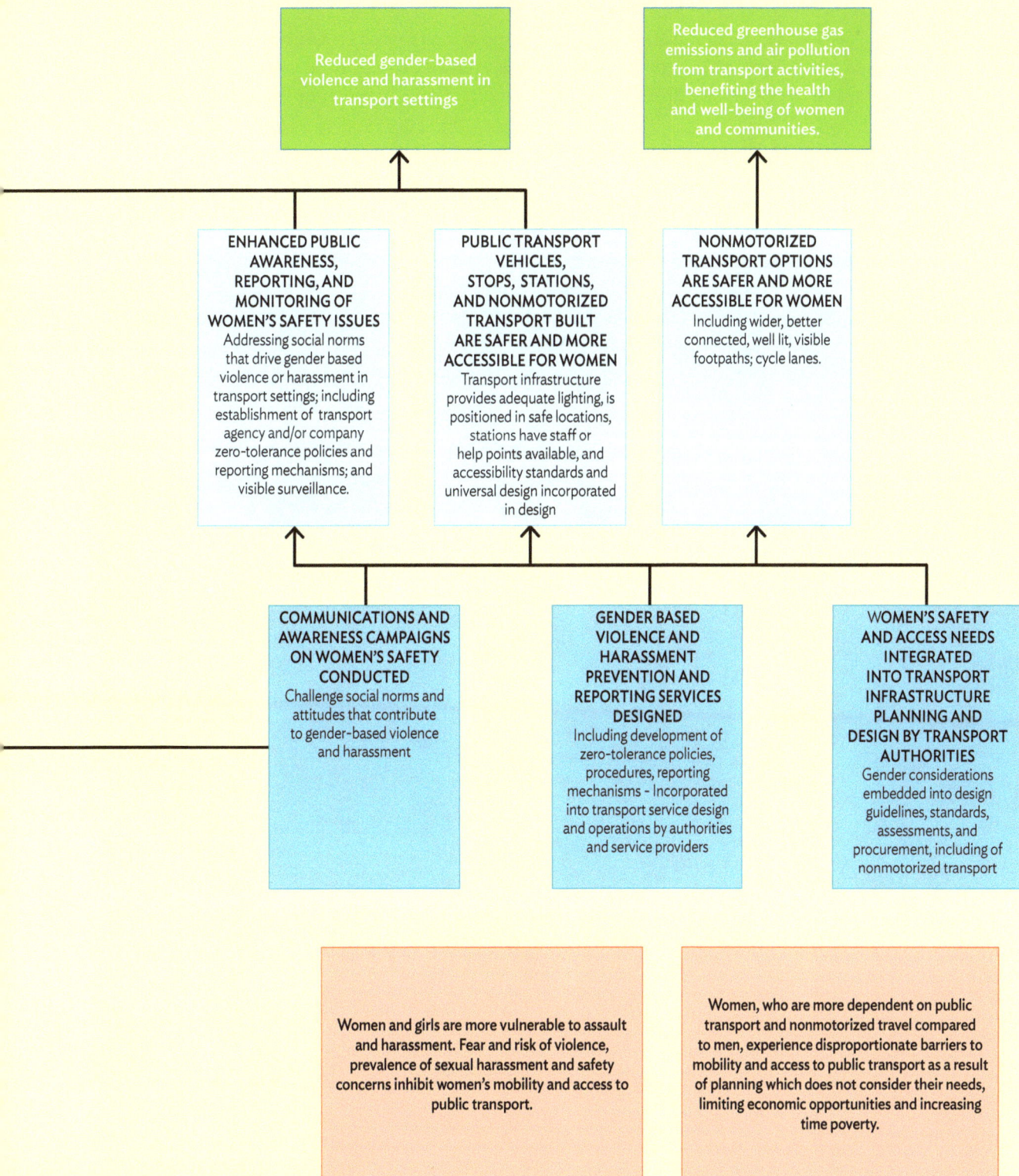

Reduced gender-based violence and harassment in transport settings

Reduced greenhouse gas emissions and air pollution from transport activities, benefiting the health and well-being of women and communities.

ENHANCED PUBLIC AWARENESS, REPORTING, AND MONITORING OF WOMEN'S SAFETY ISSUES
Addressing social norms that drive gender based violence or harassment in transport settings; including establishment of transport agency and/or company zero-tolerance policies and reporting mechanisms; and visible surveillance.

PUBLIC TRANSPORT VEHICLES, STOPS, STATIONS, AND NONMOTORIZED TRANSPORT BUILT ARE SAFER AND MORE ACCESSIBLE FOR WOMEN
Transport infrastructure provides adequate lighting, is positioned in safe locations, stations have staff or help points available, and accessibility standards and universal design incorporated in design

NONMOTORIZED TRANSPORT OPTIONS ARE SAFER AND MORE ACCESSIBLE FOR WOMEN
Including wider, better connected, well lit, visible footpaths; cycle lanes.

COMMUNICATIONS AND AWARENESS CAMPAIGNS ON WOMEN'S SAFETY CONDUCTED
Challenge social norms and attitudes that contribute to gender-based violence and harassment

GENDER BASED VIOLENCE AND HARASSMENT PREVENTION AND REPORTING SERVICES DESIGNED
Including development of zero-tolerance policies, procedures, reporting mechanisms - Incorporated into transport service design and operations by authorities and service providers

WOMEN'S SAFETY AND ACCESS NEEDS INTEGRATED INTO TRANSPORT INFRASTRUCTURE PLANNING AND DESIGN BY TRANSPORT AUTHORITIES
Gender considerations embedded into design guidelines, standards, assessments, and procurement, including of nonmotorized transport

Women and girls are more vulnerable to assault and harassment. Fear and risk of violence, prevalence of sexual harassment and safety concerns inhibit women's mobility and access to public transport.

Women, who are more dependent on public transport and nonmotorized travel compared to men, experience disproportionate barriers to mobility and access to public transport as a result of planning which does not consider their needs, limiting economic opportunities and increasing time poverty.

Assumptions

- Women are meaningfully involved in transport planning and design which leads to improvements in access and safety for all groups of women such as adolescent girls, elderly women, women with disabilities, low income groups, women entrepreneurs, and women-headed households. Similarly, gender analyses incorporate the views of women in all their diversity, where they are given the space and possibility to research and articulate the female perspective.
- The public considers violence against women in transport issues to be a serious issue and is willing to learn about how to reduce incidences of violence and change attitudes and behavior.
- Government institutions and travel companies have the time, interest, and budget to address women's needs in transport infrastructure, schedules, routes, and fare structures.
- Transport companies can make changes to suit women's travel needs—including women with disabilities—while at the same time being commercially viable.
- Alternations to make traveling safer such as lighting, help points, and readily available staff, can deter perpetrators of violence from committing crimes.
- Transport infrastructure such as help points and streetlights are adequately maintained and functioning.

Risks

- Decision-makers treat gender action plans and gender designs as "additional" elements and not as an integral part of the project, which may result in delays or non-implementation of gender features.
- Women employed in travel companies experience workplace discrimination and harassment, and/or are unable to balance paid work responsibilities with unpaid care, leading to poor retention and slow career progression.

Navigating everyday journeys. A subtle portrayal of women seamlessly steering various modes of transportation, quietly shaping the daily fabric of mobility (photos by ADB).

4.3. Water, Sanitation, and Hygiene (WASH) Sector Theory of Change (Figure 3)

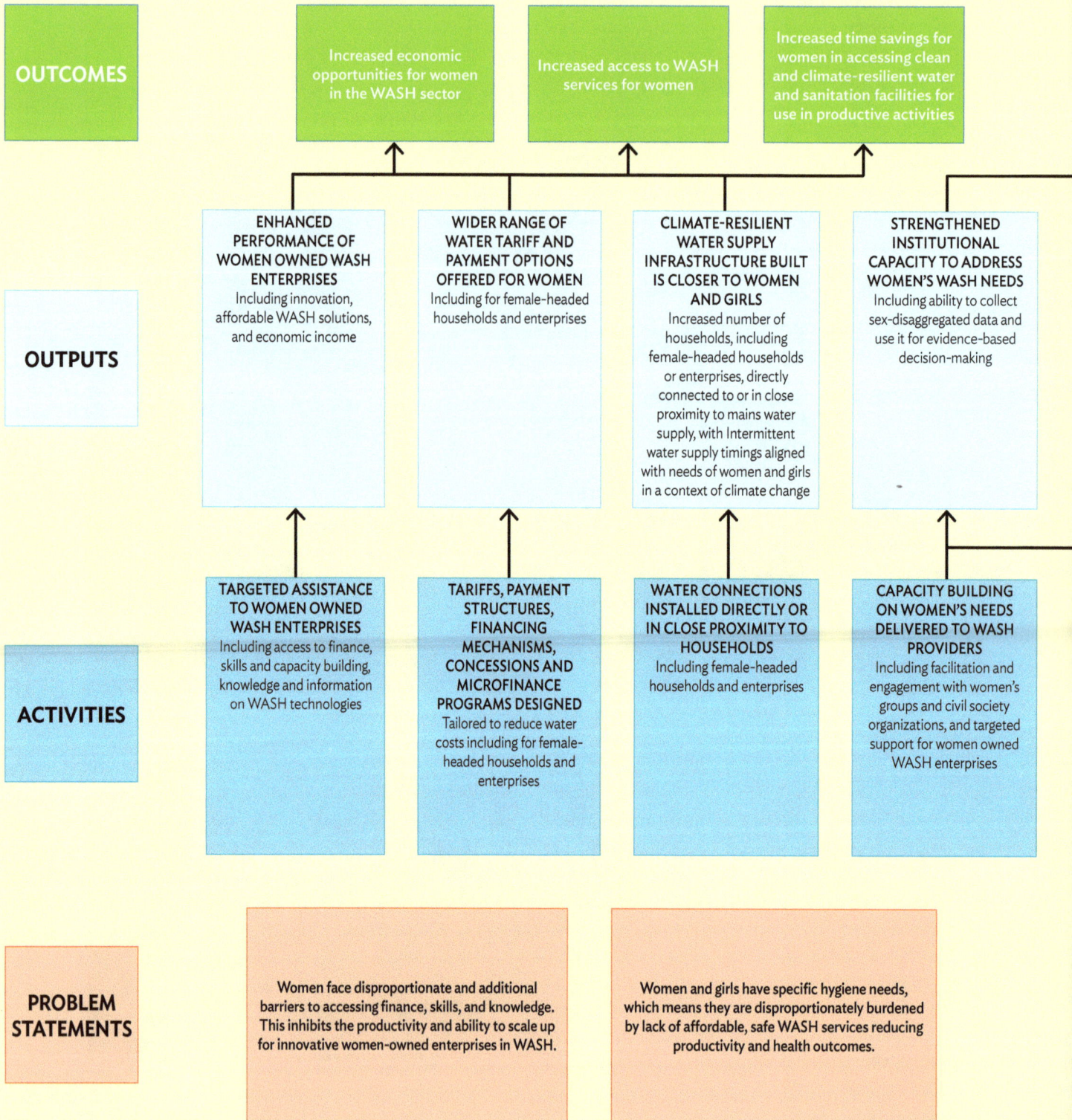

OUTCOMES

| Increased economic opportunities for women in the WASH sector | Increased access to WASH services for women | Increased time savings for women in accessing clean and climate-resilient water and sanitation facilities for use in productive activities |

OUTPUTS

| ENHANCED PERFORMANCE OF WOMEN OWNED WASH ENTERPRISES | WIDER RANGE OF WATER TARIFF AND PAYMENT OPTIONS OFFERED FOR WOMEN | CLIMATE-RESILIENT WATER SUPPLY INFRASTRUCTURE BUILT IS CLOSER TO WOMEN AND GIRLS | STRENGTHENED INSTITUTIONAL CAPACITY TO ADDRESS WOMEN'S WASH NEEDS |
| Including innovation, affordable WASH solutions, and economic income | Including for female-headed households and enterprises | Increased number of households, including female-headed households or enterprises, directly connected to or in close proximity to mains water supply, with Intermittent water supply timings aligned with needs of women and girls in a context of climate change | Including ability to collect sex-disaggregated data and use it for evidence-based decision-making |

ACTIVITIES

| TARGETED ASSISTANCE TO WOMEN OWNED WASH ENTERPRISES | TARIFFS, PAYMENT STRUCTURES, FINANCING MECHANISMS, CONCESSIONS AND MICROFINANCE PROGRAMS DESIGNED | WATER CONNECTIONS INSTALLED DIRECTLY OR IN CLOSE PROXIMITY TO HOUSEHOLDS | CAPACITY BUILDING ON WOMEN'S NEEDS DELIVERED TO WASH PROVIDERS |
| Including access to finance, skills and capacity building, knowledge and information on WASH technologies | Tailored to reduce water costs including for female-headed households and enterprises | Including female-headed households and enterprises | Including facilitation and engagement with women's groups and civil society organizations, and targeted support for women owned WASH enterprises |

PROBLEM STATEMENTS

| Women face disproportionate and additional barriers to accessing finance, skills, and knowledge. This inhibits the productivity and ability to scale up for innovative women-owned enterprises in WASH. | Women and girls have specific hygiene needs, which means they are disproportionately burdened by lack of affordable, safe WASH services reducing productivity and health outcomes. |

Source: Compiled by authors.

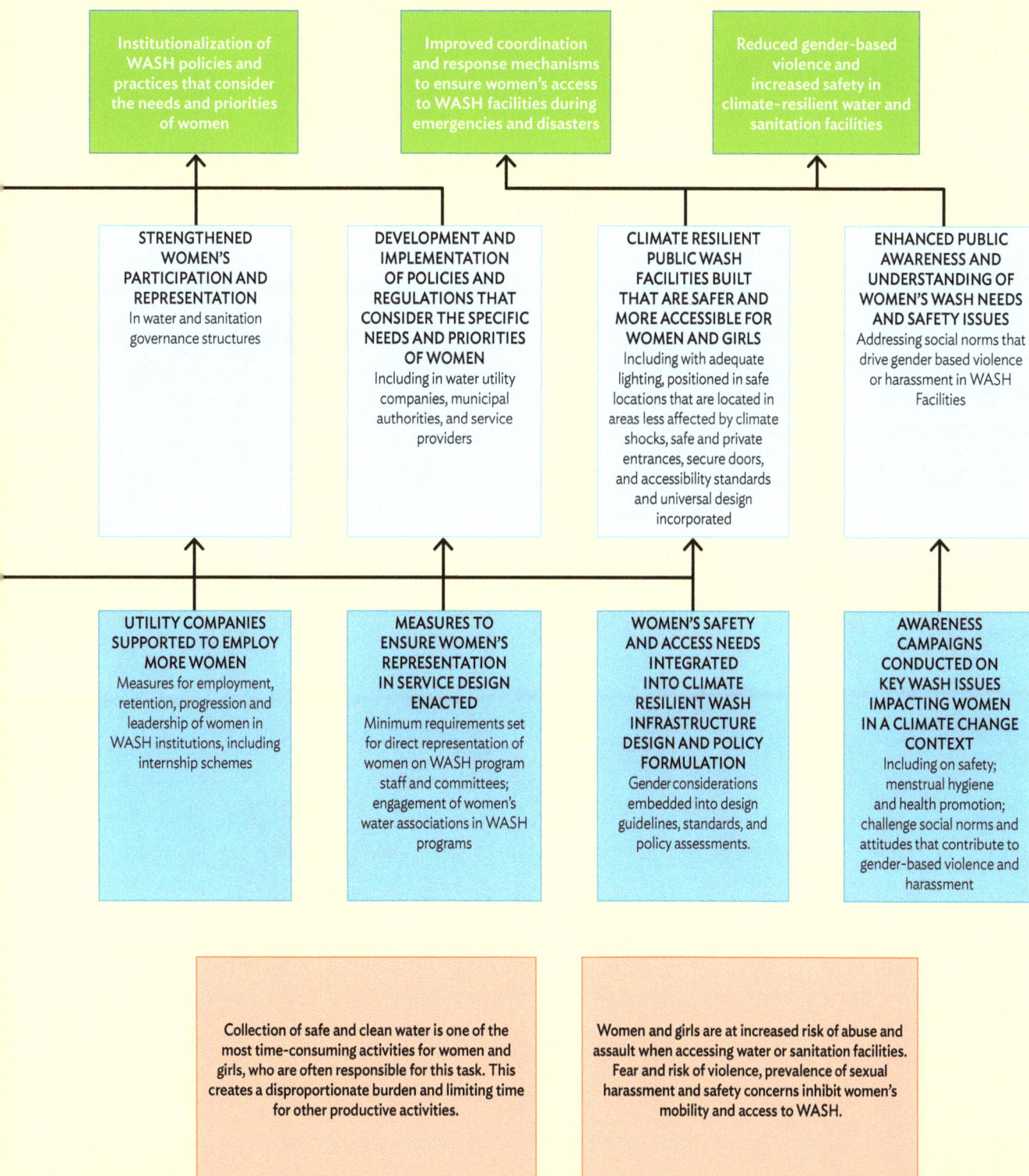

Institutionalization of WASH policies and practices that consider the needs and priorities of women

Improved coordination and response mechanisms to ensure women's access to WASH facilities during emergencies and disasters

Reduced gender-based violence and increased safety in climate-resilient water and sanitation facilities

STRENGTHENED WOMEN'S PARTICIPATION AND REPRESENTATION
In water and sanitation governance structures

DEVELOPMENT AND IMPLEMENTATION OF POLICIES AND REGULATIONS THAT CONSIDER THE SPECIFIC NEEDS AND PRIORITIES OF WOMEN
Including in water utility companies, municipal authorities, and service providers

CLIMATE RESILIENT PUBLIC WASH FACILITIES BUILT THAT ARE SAFER AND MORE ACCESSIBLE FOR WOMEN AND GIRLS
Including with adequate lighting, positioned in safe locations that are located in areas less affected by climate shocks, safe and private entrances, secure doors, and accessibility standards and universal design incorporated

ENHANCED PUBLIC AWARENESS AND UNDERSTANDING OF WOMEN'S WASH NEEDS AND SAFETY ISSUES
Addressing social norms that drive gender based violence or harassment in WASH Facilities

UTILITY COMPANIES SUPPORTED TO EMPLOY MORE WOMEN
Measures for employment, retention, progression and leadership of women in WASH institutions, including internship schemes

MEASURES TO ENSURE WOMEN'S REPRESENTATION IN SERVICE DESIGN ENACTED
Minimum requirements set for direct representation of women on WASH program staff and committees; engagement of women's water associations in WASH programs

WOMEN'S SAFETY AND ACCESS NEEDS INTEGRATED INTO CLIMATE RESILIENT WASH INFRASTRUCTURE DESIGN AND POLICY FORMULATION
Gender considerations embedded into design guidelines, standards, and policy assessments.

AWARENESS CAMPAIGNS CONDUCTED ON KEY WASH ISSUES IMPACTING WOMEN IN A CLIMATE CHANGE CONTEXT
Including on safety; menstrual hygiene and health promotion; challenge social norms and attitudes that contribute to gender-based violence and harassment

Collection of safe and clean water is one of the most time-consuming activities for women and girls, who are often responsible for this task. This creates a disproportionate burden and limiting time for other productive activities.

Women and girls are at increased risk of abuse and assault when accessing water or sanitation facilities. Fear and risk of violence, prevalence of sexual harassment and safety concerns inhibit women's mobility and access to WASH.

Assumptions

- Women are meaningfully involved in WASH planning and design which leads to improvements in access for all groups of women such as adolescent girls, elderly women, women with disabilities, low income groups, women entrepreneurs, and women-headed households. Similarly, gender analyses incorporate the views of women in all their diversity, where they are given the space and possibility to research and articulate the female perspective.
- The participation and representation of women in water and sanitation governance structures lead to an increase in decision-making by women and making decisions that disproportionately benefit women.
- Government institutions and utility companies have the time, interest, and budget to address women's WASH needs.
- The public considers women's WASH needs and safety to be a serious issue and is willing to learn, change attitudes, and shift behavior.
- Utility companies can make changes to suit women's WASH needs while continuing to be commercially viable.
- Women's involvement in service design leads to improvements in accessibility and safety for all groups of women such as adolescent girls, elderly women, or women with disabilities.
- Policies and regulations that consider the specific needs and priorities of women in the WASH sector are implemented and enforced.
- Women want to and can be employed in utility companies, considering attitudes from spouses or male relatives and balancing unpaid care work duties.
- Public WASH facilities are adequately maintained and are functioning efficiently.

Risks

→ Decision-makers treat gender action plans and gender designs as "additional" elements and not as an integral part of the project, which may result in delays or non-implementation of gender features.

→ Women employed in utility companies experience workplace discrimination and harassment, and/or are unable to balance paid work responsibilities with unpaid care, leading to poor retention and slow career progression.

Balancing roles. A glimpse into women nurturing families, ensuring clean water and sanitation access, and playing a vital role in daily life and community infrastructure (photos by ADB).

4.4. Energy Sector Theory of Change (Figure 4)

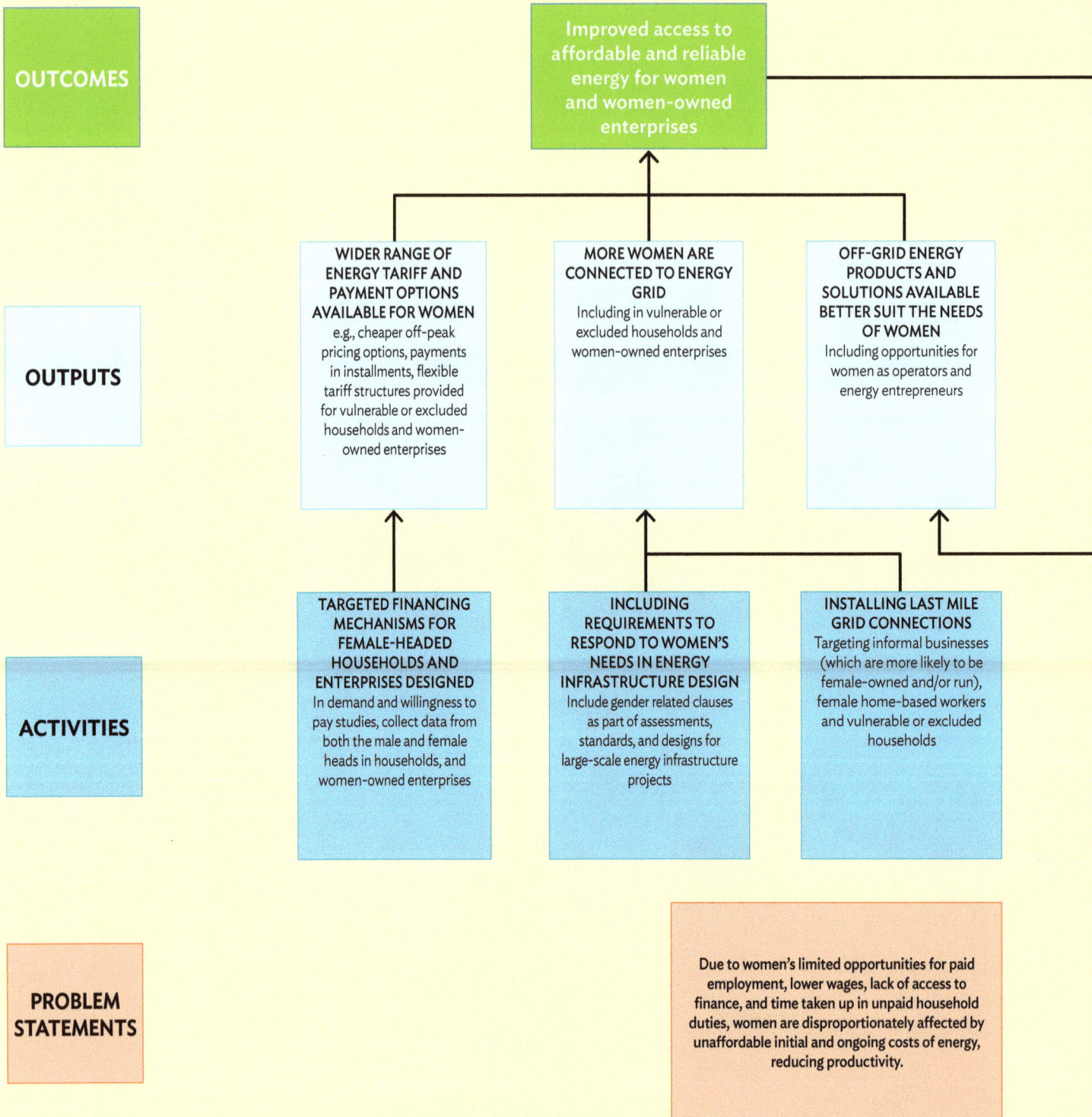

OUTCOMES

Improved access to affordable and reliable energy for women and women-owned enterprises

OUTPUTS

WIDER RANGE OF ENERGY TARIFF AND PAYMENT OPTIONS AVAILABLE FOR WOMEN
e.g., cheaper off-peak pricing options, payments in installments, flexible tariff structures provided for vulnerable or excluded households and women-owned enterprises

MORE WOMEN ARE CONNECTED TO ENERGY GRID
Including in vulnerable or excluded households and women-owned enterprises

OFF-GRID ENERGY PRODUCTS AND SOLUTIONS AVAILABLE BETTER SUIT THE NEEDS OF WOMEN
Including opportunities for women as operators and energy entrepreneurs

ACTIVITIES

TARGETED FINANCING MECHANISMS FOR FEMALE-HEADED HOUSEHOLDS AND ENTERPRISES DESIGNED
In demand and willingness to pay studies, collect data from both the male and female heads in households, and women-owned enterprises

INCLUDING REQUIREMENTS TO RESPOND TO WOMEN'S NEEDS IN ENERGY INFRASTRUCTURE DESIGN
Include gender related clauses as part of assessments, standards, and designs for large-scale energy infrastructure projects

INSTALLING LAST MILE GRID CONNECTIONS
Targeting informal businesses (which are more likely to be female-owned and/or run), female home-based workers and vulnerable or excluded households

PROBLEM STATEMENTS

Due to women's limited opportunities for paid employment, lower wages, lack of access to finance, and time taken up in unpaid household duties, women are disproportionately affected by unaffordable initial and ongoing costs of energy, reducing productivity.

Source: Compiled by authors.

Increased employment and entrepreneurship opportunities for women in the energy sector

STRENGTHENED INSTITUTIONAL CAPACITY TO ADDRESS WOMEN'S ENERGY NEEDS
Including ability to collect sex-disaggregated data and use it for evidence-based decision-making

MORE WOMEN ARE TRAINED IN ENERGY MANAGEMENT
Including skills for employment in energy supply chain, for example in sales, marketing, and distribution of new products and services.

MORE WOMEN ARE EMPLOYED IN PROJECT'S ENERGY INFRASTRUCTURE CONSTRUCTION
Including women from areas local to infrastructure investments

INTEGRATING WOMEN'S NEEDS INTO OFF-GRID ENERGY SOLUTION DESIGN
Targeting women's needs and concerns in developing and accessing off-grid options and distribution networks

CAPACITY BUILDING ON WOMEN'S NEEDS DELIVERED TO ENERGY COMPANIES
Including policymakers, planners, engineers, and project managers, to enhance their understanding of gender issues and their integration into energy infrastructure

TRAINING WOMEN IN ENERGY INFRASTRUCTURE CONSTRUCTION, OPERATION AND MAINTENANCE JOBS
Including training and skills for renewable energy projects; and roles across energy supply chain such as sales and distribution

SUPPORTING ENERGY COMPANIES TO EMPLOY MORE WOMEN
Measures for employment, retention, progression and leadership of women in energy companies, including use of context appropriate quotas for minimum representation

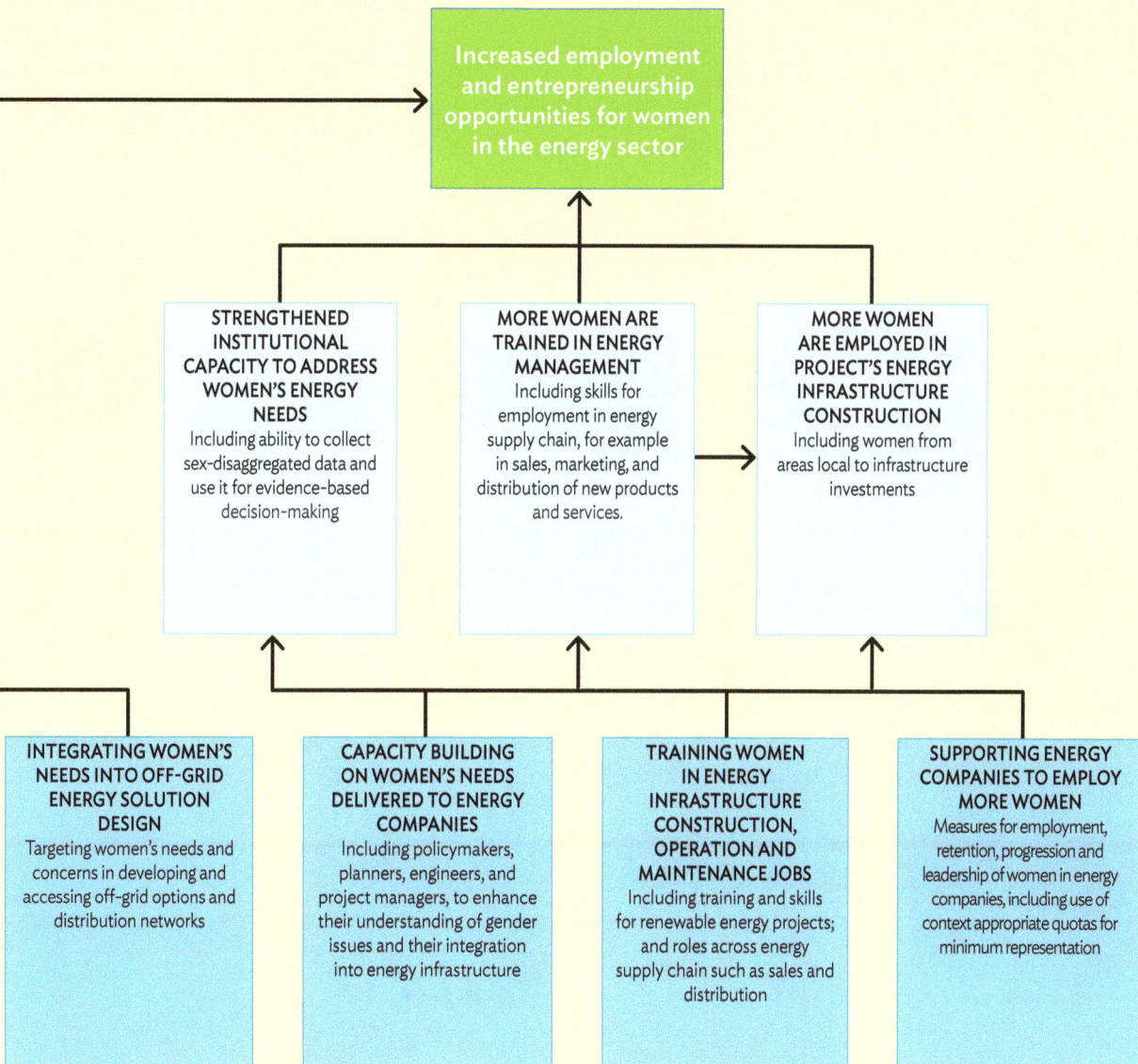

Due to household and care responsibilities of women and girls, as well as home-based workers being mainly women, nonexistent or irregular electricity supply can considerably increase their time poverty, reducing the number of productive hours in a day and increase the unpaid domestic work burden

There is a lack of recognition of the different ways in which women and men access and use energy. Women are also underrepresented in the energy sector. This leads to energy infrastructure projects which do not meet women's needs and limits their economic opportunities

Assumptions

- Women are meaningfully involved in energy planning and design which leads to improvements in access for all groups of women including adolescent girls, elderly women, women with disabilities, low-income groups, women entrepreneurs, and women-headed households. Similarly, gender analyses incorporate the views of women in all their diversity, where they are given the space and possibility to research and articulate the female perspective.
- Women want to and can be employed in energy management and energy infrastructure construction roles, considering attitudes from spouses or male relatives and balancing unpaid care work duties.
- Government institutions and energy companies have the time, interest, and budget to address women's needs in energy design and infrastructure.
- The energy grid can support a surge in users, including female-headed households and women-owned enterprises.
- Energy solutions are well maintained and functioning efficiently, resulting in improved access to affordable and reliable energy for women and women-owned enterprises.
- Off-grid energy products and solutions available will result in increased access to energy for women and women-owned enterprises.

Energizing progress. A glimpse into the diverse roles of women in sustainable energy, quietly advancing clean infrastructure solutions for a brighter future (photos by ADB).

Risks

- Decision-makers treat gender action plans and gender designs as "additional" elements and not as an integral part of the project, which may result in delays or non-implementation of gender features.
- Women employed in energy companies experience workplace discrimination and harassment, and/or are unable to balance paid work responsibilities with unpaid care, leading to poor retention and slow career progression.
- Women working in energy infrastructure construction roles experience health and safety risks.

5 RECOMMENDATIONS

This section provides some general recommendations summarizing how the information and guidance provided in this paper can be used. The recommendations recap and highlight some of the key messages and considerations proposed in this paper. They aim to support project officers in providing a starting point for how they can better incorporate gender equality and women's empowerment into ADB infrastructure projects.

1. **Identify opportunities** to promote gender equality and women's empowerment at the start of a project.

   (a) Ensure a thorough gender analysis is conducted identifying key issues related to women and girls in a project's context.

   (b) Assess the type of project against the corresponding sector theory of change presented in section 4 to see what outcomes and outputs could be adapted to your project, given the risks and assumptions. Ensure selected activities are firmly grounded in analysis and follow a logical results chain.

   (c) Refer to Annex 1 and the case studies in Annex 2 for example outcomes, including how existing proposed outcomes could be modified to address gender equality and women's empowerment.

   (d) Think broadly about the role of women and girls in the proposed infrastructure project, including active stakeholders, employees, entrepreneurs, contractors, decision-makers as well and the end users of infrastructure (Menon 2019).

2. **Build consensus** and awareness within project teams and with clients on the value of gender equality and women's empowerment.

   (a) Engage clients early on the opportunities to incorporate gender equality-related outcomes. Use the business case presented in section 2.2 to convince clients to review and rethink project designs and business models. This will be an iterative process, engaging with different disciplines at all stages of the project cycle. Identify synergies with the client, helping them build on their existing commitments to gender equality (including policy commitments, laws, compliance, or environmental, social, and corporate governance (ESG) initiatives).

(b) Engage internal ADB teams across disciplines to build a common understanding of gender equality-related ambitions, opportunities, and considerations of risks that may prevent desired outcomes or outputs on gender equality or women's empowerment. Draw on the experience and expertise across teams within ADB, including the gender team. This could include, for example, holding a cross team brainstorm on the theory of change in terms of gender equality and women's empowerment.

3. **Lock in ambition on gender equality** issues identified by capturing them in project documents, the gender action plan, DMF, and measurement framework.

   (a) Ensure that the ambitions and objectives on gender equality and women's empowerment are identified at the beginning of a project through effective gender analysis and that these ambitions and objectives are advanced by incorporating actions across the project cycle. This includes ensuring actions are captured in the gender action plan.

   (b) Utilize the relevant TOC related to your project from section 4 and causal pathways presented in section 4.4 to identify contextually appropriate and relevant project outcomes that are achievable and to identify what would be required to achieve these outcomes. This should include a review of all proposed project activities and objectives, including those that may not be focused on gender equality or women's empowerment, to identify how these could be recalibrated to target women or excluded groups.

   (c) Identify key opportunities for gender equality impact and Incorporate these opportunities in the design of the project results chain and DMF, including brainstorming opportunities in cross-disciplinary teams.

   (d) Select suitable indicators based on Annex 1. Identify what would be needed to gather this data, including whether existing channels can provide this data, or if new data needs to be gathered.

MENU OF INDICATORS

This annex provides a menu of indicators corresponding to outputs and outcomes presented in the sector theory of change diagrams (section 4). These are provided to enable the design of a design and monitoring framework (DMF) that incorporates gender inclusion indicators and supports gender tagging of ADB projects. Project teams should note that:

- Indicators need to be adapted on a project-by-project basis to account for sector specifics, local context, and baselines ensuring eventual indicators are specific, measurable, achievable, relevant, and time-bound (SMART) as per DMF guidance. Staff should use a gender analysis to consider if data is to be collected from groups of women such as women with disabilities, elderly women, adolescent girls, and/or women living below the poverty line.
- ADB project teams should involve key stakeholders in finalizing and agreeing on indicators in a project, and these tables are intended to provide a starting point.
- The level of impact is illustrated for reference purposes (concerning the levels of impact presented in section 3.1). When selecting indicators at different levels of impact, consider where it may be useful to measure institutional metrics such as policies, standards, and requirements related to gender equality and women's empowerment, as well as indicators that measure number of women impacted, for example.
- Correspondence to ADB's Operational Priority 2 tracking Indicators has been indicated.

Table A1.1: Urban Sector Indicators

	Statement	Indicator	Level of Impact	Source	Corresponding ADB Tracking Indicator
Outcome	Improved access to affordable municipal services for women	Number of women who access different types of municipal services	Basic needs and priorities	Program M&E	2.4.1 Time-saving or gender-responsive infrastructure assets and/or services established or improved
	Increased time savings for women for use in productive activities	Average travel time to markets, financial services, and places of employment by women	Basic needs and priorities	Program M&E	2.4 Women and girls with increased time savings
		Average travel time to schools and health services by women, men, girls, and boys, by mode of transport	Basic needs and priorities	Program M&E	2.4 Women and girls with increased time savings

continued on next page

Table A1.1, *continued*

	Statement	Indicator	Level of Impact	Source	Corresponding ADB Tracking Indicator
Outcome	Improved mobility for women, including women with disabilities	Number of additional school enrollments by girls and boys because of improved transport facilities and services	Empowerment	Program M&E	2.1.4 Women and girls benefiting from new or improved infrastructure
		Number of women with increased incomes because of improved transport facilities and services	Empowerment	Program M&E	2.4 Women and girls with increased time savings
		Number and percentage of women who access employment or better income opportunities because of improved transport infrastructure and services	Empowerment	Program M&E	2.4 Women and girls with increased time savings
	Women and girls feel safer to use urban spaces and public transport	Number of physical and sexual assaults on public transport reported by women and girls (including by female staff)	Basic needs and priorities	Program M&E	2.4.1 Time-saving or gender-responsive infrastructure assets and/or services established or improved 2.2.3 Solutions to prevent or address gender-based violence implemented
		Women's and girls' perceptions of physical safety in public spaces because of street lighting.	Basic needs and priorities	Program M&E	—
		Number of street markets that include women vendors' safety concerns in design	Basic needs and priorities	Program M&E	2.4.1 Time-saving or gender-responsive infrastructure assets and/or services established or improved
		Women's perceptions of safety when using modes of public transport	Basic needs and priorities	Program M&E	—
	Improved access to affordable housing and homeownership for women	Number of women with access to land or housing title, individual or joint	Empowerment	Program M&E	2.4.1 Time-saving or gender-responsive infrastructure assets and/or services established or improved
		Number of women with increased access to quality housing	Empowerment	Program M&E	2.1.4 Women and girls benefiting from new or improved infrastructure
	Women recover faster from the economic impacts of climate risks and disasters	Average time that women take to recover from economic impacts of climate disasters	Empowerment	Program M&E	2.5 Women and girls with increased resilience to climate change, disasters, and other external shocks

continued on next page

Table A1.1, *continued*

	Statement	Indicator	Level of Impact	Source	Corresponding ADB Tracking Indicator
Output	Municipal institutions better equipped to meet the needs of women: utility companies better equipped to identify and respond to the needs of women	Percentage of utility companies that can identify and respond to the needs of women	Shifting institutions and cultural and social norms	Program M&E	—
	Municipal services built to meet the needs of women: physical supply, proximity, and pricing of utilities designed to reflect barriers and needs of women, including female-headed households and women-owned enterprises	Number of women who perceive that municipal services meet their needs	Basic needs and priorities	Program M&E	2.4.1 Time-saving or gender-responsive infrastructure assets and/or services established or improved
	Spatial planning of housing and services built to accommodate women's needs: design and proximity of infrastructure, services, and amenities reflect the economic and social needs of women	Percentage of women who perceive that spatial planning of housing and services reflects their economic and social needs	Basic needs and priorities	Program M&E	2.1.4. Women and girls benefiting from new or improved infrastructure
	Planning policy addresses women's needs: integrated urban development plans or municipal plans produced or approved that better reflect the needs of women and girls guide future development	Percentage of integrated urban development plans or municipal plans produced that reflect evidence of the needs of women and girls	Shifting institutions and cultural and social norms	Program M&E	2.3.2 Measures of gender equality supported in implementation

continued on next page

Table A1.1, *continued*

	Statement	Indicator	Level of Impact	Source	Corresponding ADB Tracking Indicator
Output	Transport infrastructure constructed supports women's travel needs: tailored transport schedules, fee structures, and network coverage implemented which reflect the needs of women, and use innovative digital technologies	Percentage of women who perceive that transport infrastructure constructed supports their travel needs	Basic needs and priorities	Program M&E	2.4.1 Time-saving or gender-responsive infrastructure assets and/or services established or improved
	Transport operators trained on women's and girls' safety: transport operators better equipped to respond to incidents	Percentage of transport operator staff and contractors that have received basic training on women's and girls' safety	Shifting institutions and cultural and social norms	Program M&E	2.2.3. Solutions to prevent or address gender-based violence implemented
	Infrastructure constructed reflects women's and girls' safety concerns: sight lines, improved lighting, safe and private entrances, secure doors, and passive surveillance implemented in stations, urban spaces, and wash facilities	Percentage of women and girls who perceive that infrastructure constructed reflects their safety concerns	Basic needs and priorities	Program M&E	2.1.4. Women and girls benefiting from new or improved infrastructure
	Housing built is more affordable to women: housing developments offer a variety of tenure types and financing arrangements tailored for female-headed households	Number of women with access to housing finance options that include incremental building	Empowerment	Program M&E	2.4.1 Time-saving or gender-responsive infrastructure assets and/or services established or improved

continued on next page

Table A1.1, *continued*

	Statement	Indicator	Level of Impact	Source	Corresponding ADB Tracking Indicator
Output	Housing built supports women's economic activities: design of housing reflects home-based working and care needs of women and men	Number of new housing units designed to reflect the needs of women home-based workers	Empowerment	Program M&E	2.4.1 Time-saving or gender-responsive infrastructure assets and/or services established or improved
	Emergency shelters that meet the needs of women built: shelter infrastructure designed to be inclusive of women, including women with disabilities	Percentage of women who perceive that emergency shelters meet their needs	Basic needs and priorities	Program M&E	2.5.2 Climate- and disaster-resilient infrastructure assets and/or services for women and girls established or improved 2.1.4. Women and girls benefiting from new or improved infrastructure
		Percentage of emergency shelters that are designed that reflect evidence of women's needs, including women with disabilities	Basic needs and priorities	Program M&E	2.5.2. Climate- and disaster-resilient infrastructure assets and/or services for women and girls established or improved
	Disaster and livelihood recovery plans include measures for women: disaster recovery and livelihood restoration plans delivered that support women's distinct recovery needs	Percentage of disaster and livelihood recovery plans that include measures for women, including their distinct recovery needs	Shifting institutions and cultural and social norms	Program M&E	2.5.1 Community-based initiatives to build the resilience of women and girls to external shocks implemented 2.5.3 Savings and insurance schemes for women implemented or established 2.5.4 Dedicated crisis-responding social assistance schemes for women and girls implemented or established
	Early warning systems more effectively reach women using innovative technologies: early warning systems reach more people, including women and girls	Percentage of disaster and livelihood recovery plans that include measures for women and girls, including their distinct recovery needs	Shifting institutions and cultural and social norms	Program M&E	2.5.1 Community-based initiatives to build the resilience of women and girls to external shocks implemented 2.5.2 Climate- and disaster-resilient infrastructure assets and/or services for women and girls established or improved

M&E = monitoring and evaluation.
Source: Compiled for this report.

Table A1.2: Transport Indicators

	Statement	Indicator	Level of Impact	Source	Corresponding ADB Tracking Indicator
Outcome	Increased accessibility, affordability, and efficiency of transport options for women, including women with disabilities	Average travel time to markets, financial services, and places of employment by women	Basic needs and priorities	Program M&E	2.4 Women and girls with increased time savings
		Number of women with increased incomes because of improved transport facilities and services	Empowerment	Program M&E	2.1.4. Women and girls benefiting from new or improved infrastructure
		Number and percentage of women who access employment or better income opportunities because of improved transport infrastructure and services	Empowerment	Program M&E	2.1.4. Women and girls benefiting from new or improved infrastructure
		Average travel time to schools and health services by women and girls, by mode of transport	Basic needs and priorities	Program M&E	2.4 Women and girls with increased time savings
		Number of additional school enrolments by girls and boys because of improved transport facilities and services	Empowerment	Program M&E	2.1.4. Women and girls benefiting from new or improved infrastructure
	Reduced gender-based violence and harassment in transport settings	Percentage of women and girls who perceive modes of public transport to be safe	Basic needs and priorities	Program M&E	2.2.3. Solutions to prevent or address gender-based violence implemented
		Number of physical and sexual assaults on public transport reported by women and girls (including by female staff)	Basic needs and priorities	Program M&E	—
Output	Public transport vehicles, stops, and stations built are safer and more accessible for women and girls, including women/girls with disabilities: transport infrastructure provides adequate lighting, is positioned in safe locations, stations have staff or help points available, and accessibility standards and universal design incorporated	Percentage of women and girls who perceive that public transport vehicles, stops, and stations are safe and accessible	Basic needs and priorities	Program M&E	2.4.1 Time-saving or gender-responsive infrastructure assets and/or services established or improved

continued on next page

Table A1.2, *continued*

	Statement	Indicator	Level of Impact	Source	Corresponding ADB Tracking Indicator
Output		Percentage of women with disabilities who perceive that public transport vehicles, stops, and stations are accessible	Basic needs and priorities	Program M&E	2.1.4 Women and girls benefiting from new or improved infrastructure 2.4.2 Child and elderly care services established or improved
		Percentage of elderly women who perceive that public transport vehicles, stops, and stations are accessible	Basic needs and priorities	Program M&E	2.4.2 Child and elderly care services established or improved
	Fare structures are tailored to women's journeys: fare systems enable transit or multi-stop journeys to respond to women's more complex travel patterns	Percentage of women who perceive that fare structures are tailored to their everyday journeys	Basic needs and priorities	Program M&E	2.1.4. Women and girls benefiting from new or improved infrastructure
	Approved and implemented routes and schedules that reflect women's travel needs: public transport schedules and routes address and/or reflect the travel needs of women	Percentage of women who perceive that public transport schedules and routes address their travel needs	Basic needs and priorities	Program M&E	2.4.1 Time-saving or gender-responsive infrastructure assets and/or services established or improved
	Strengthened institutional capacity to address women's needs: including the ability to collect sex-disaggregated data and use it for evidence-based decision-making, and a confidential mechanism to report gender-based violence incidences on transport	Number of staff in water companies enrolled in technical and skills development training on addressing women's needs	Shifting institutions and cultural and social norms	Program M&E	2..2.3 Solutions to prevent or address gender-based violence implemented

continued on next page

Table A1.2, *continued*

	Statement	Indicator	Level of Impact	Source	Corresponding ADB Tracking Indicator
Output	Enhanced public awareness and understanding of women's and girls' safety issues: addressing social norms that drive gender-based violence or harassment in transport settings	Percentage of men and boys in the community that have an awareness and understanding of women's transport safety issues	Shifting institutions and cultural and social norms	Program M&E	2.2.3. Solutions to prevent or address gender-based violence implemented

M&E = monitoring and evaluation
Source: Compiled for this report.

Table A1.3: Water, Sanitation, and Hygiene (WASH) Indicators

	Statement	Indicator	Level of Impact	Source	Corresponding ADB Tracking Indicator
Outcome	Improved coordination and response mechanisms to ensure women's and girls' access to water, sanitation, and hygiene (WASH) facilities during emergencies and disasters	Number of crop insurance schemes for disaster and climate emergencies designed or targeted to women farmers	Basic needs and priorities	Program M&E	2.5.3 Savings and insurance schemes for women implemented or established
		Number of women accessing social protection during economic shocks	Basic needs and priorities/ Empowerment	Program M&E	2.5 Women and girls with increased resilience to climate change, disasters, and other external shocks
		Number of social protection schemes established targeted at women during economic shocks	Shifting institutions and cultural and social norms	Program M&E	2.5.4 Dedicated crisis-responding social assistance schemes for women and girls implemented or established
		Number of women and girls who perceive that coordination and response mechanisms are sufficient in ensuring their access to WASH facilities—including for menstrual hygiene management—during emergencies and disasters	Basic needs and priorities	Program M&E	—
		Local women's group organized and trained on risk mapping	Empowerment	Program M&E	OP 2.5.1 Community-based initiatives to build the resilience of women and girls to external shocks implemented
		Community-based women's groups mobilized to educate communities in disaster-prone urban settings in advocating for their emergency and disaster resilience priorities	Empowerment/ Shifting institutions and cultural and social norms	Program M&E	OP 2.5.1 Community-based initiatives to build the resilience of women and girls to external shocks implemented

continued on next page

53

Table A1.3, *continued*

		Statement	Indicator	Level of Impact	Source	Corresponding ADB Tracking Indicator
Outcome		Reduced gender-based violence and increased safety in climate-resilient water and sanitation facilities	Number of women and girls who perceive that climate-resilient WASH facilities are safe	Basic needs and priorities	Program M&E	2.2.3 Solutions to prevent or address gender-based violence implemented (number) 2.5.4. Dedicated crisis-responding social assistance schemes for women and girls implemented or established (number)
		Increased time savings for women and girls in accessing clean and climate-resilient water and sanitation facilities	Amount of time spent (or travel distance) by women and girls to gather clean and climate-resilient water and sanitation facilities for domestic use.	Basic needs and priorities	WHO Household Energy Database	2.4 Women and girls with increased time savings (number)
		Enhanced support for women-owned enterprises in WASH	Average time for women to start a WASH business (days)	Empowerment	Program M&E	—
			Women-owned or -led WASH SME loan accounts opened or women-owned or -led WASH SME end borrowers reached (number)	Empowerment	Program M&E	2.1.2 Women opening new accounts
		Increased access to WASH services for women and girls, including women/girls with disabilities	Proportion of women and girls using reliable and affordable basic drinking water services (%), disaggregated by rural and urban and by disability status	Basic needs and priorities	World Bank World Development Indicators, service providers	2.1.4 Women and girls benefiting from new or improved infrastructure (number)
			Proportion of women and girls using reliable and affordable basic sanitation services (%), disaggregated by rural and urban and by disability status	Basic needs and priorities	World Bank World Development Indicators, service providers	2.1.4 Women and girls benefiting from new or improved infrastructure (number)
			Proportion of women and girls that have menstruated in the last 12 months, aged 15–49, that use menstrual materials to capture and contain menstrual blood (e.g. pads, tampons, or cups), disaggregated by age group	Basic needs and priorities	Multiple indicator cluster surveys (MICS) program	—
Output		Wider range of water tariff and payment options is offered for women, including for female-headed households and enterprises	Number of water tariff and payment options offered for women	Basic needs and priorities	Program M&E	2.4.1 Time-saving or gender-responsive infrastructure assets and/or services established or improved (number)

continued on next page

Table A1.3, *continued*

	Statement	Indicator	Level of Impact	Source	Corresponding ADB Tracking Indicator
Output	Strengthened women's participation and representation in water and sanitation governance structures	Percentage of women who participate in water and sanitation governance structures (management, boards, committees)	Basic needs and priorities/ Empowerment	Program M&E	2.3 Women represented in decision-making structures and processes (number)
		Number of women in water companies enrolled in technical and skills development training	Empowerment	Program M&E	2.1.1 Women enrolled in TVET and other job training (number) or 2.2.1. Women and girls enrolled in STEM or nontraditional TVET (number)
		Number of women with strengthened leadership capacities	Empowerment	Program M&E	2.3.1 Women with strengthened leadership capacities (number)
		Number of women with leadership roles in water and sanitation governance structures (management, boards, committees)	Empowerment/ Shifting institutions and cultural and social norms	Program M&E	2.3 Women represented in decision-making structures and processes
	Climate resilient public WASH facilities built that are safer and more accessible for women and girls (including women and girls with disabilities) including with adequate lighting, positioned in safe locations that are in areas less affected by climate shocks, safe and private entrances, secure doors, accessibility standards and universal design incorporated, with considerations for menstrual hygiene management	Number of street markets that include women vendors' safety concerns in design	Basic needs and priorities	Program M&E	or 2.4.1. Time-saving or gender-responsive infrastructure assets and/or services established or improved (number)
		Number of women and girls with access to a safe, single-sex community, private or school toilet that is suitable for menstrual hygiene management, disaggregated by disability status	Basic needs and priorities	Program M&E	2.1.4 Women and girls benefiting from new or improved infrastructure (number)
	Strengthened institutional capacity to address women's and girls' WASH needs including the ability to collect sex-disaggregated data and use it for evidence-based decision-making	Number of institutional policies that are targeted at women's and girls' WASH needs	Shifting institutions and cultural and social norms	Program M&E	2.3.2. Measures on gender equality supported in implementation (number)

continued on next page

Table A1.3, *continued*

	Statement	Indicator	Level of Impact	Source	Corresponding ADB Tracking Indicator
Output		Percentage of staff who perceive they can address women's and girls' WASH needs	Shifting institutions and cultural and social norms	Program M&E	—
	Strengthened institutional capacity to address women's WASH needs including the ability to collect sex-disaggregated data and use it for evidence-based decision-making	Number of designed policies and regulations that consider the specific needs and priorities of women in the WASH sector	Shifting institutions and cultural and social norms	Program M&E	2.3.2. Measures on gender equality supported in implementation (number)
		Number of implemented policies and regulations that consider the specific needs and priorities of women in the WASH sector	Shifting institutions and cultural and social norms	Program M&E	2.3.2. Measures on gender equality supported in implementation (number)
	Enhanced public awareness and understanding of women's and girls' WASH needs and safety issues, including women and girls with disabilities: addressing social norms that drive gender-based violence or harassment in WASH Facilities	Percentage of men and boys in the community that have an awareness and understanding of women's WASH needs and safety issues, including women and girls with disabilities	Shifting institutions and cultural and social norms	Program M&E	2.2.3 Solutions to prevent or address gender-based violence implemented (number)
	Climate-resilient water supply infrastructure built is closer to women and girls: increased number of households, including female-headed households or enterprises, directly connected to or close to mains water supply, with intermittent water supply timings aligned with needs of women and girls in a context of climate change	Number of female-headed households directly connected to or within XXm to a mains water supply, with intermittent water supply timings aligned with the needs of women and girls in a context of climate change	Basic needs and priorities	Program M&E	2.4 Women and girls with increased time savings or 2.1.4 Women and girls benefiting from new or improved infrastructure and 2.5.2. Climate- and disaster-resilient infrastructure assets and/or services for women and girls established or improved

continued on next page

Table A1.3, *continued*

	Statement	Indicator	Level of Impact	Source	Corresponding ADB Tracking Indicator
Output		Number of women-owned enterprises directly connected to or within XXm to a mains water supply, with intermittent water supply timings aligned with the needs of women and girls in a context of climate change	Empowerment	Program M&E	2.1.4. Women and girls benefiting from new or improved infrastructure
		Revised or established a water interruption schedule designed based on needs identified by women's group	Basic needs and priorities	Program M&E	2.1.4. Women and girls benefiting from new or improved infrastructure (number)

M&E = monitoring and evaluation, MICS = multiple indicator cluster surveys, SME = small and medium-sized enterprise, STEM = science, technology, engineering, and mathematics, TVET = technical and vocational education and training, WASH = water, sanitation, and hygiene
Source: Compiled for this report.

Table A1.4: Energy Indicators

	Statement	Indicator	Level of Impact	Source	Corresponding ADB Tracking Indicator
Outcome	Improved access to affordable and reliable energy for women and women-owned enterprises	Number and percentage of families who report that household access to reliable energy has supported girls' school attendance.	Empowerment	Program M&E	2.1.4. Women and girls benefiting from new or improved infrastructure (number)
		Women and girls' respiratory infection prevalence rate.	Basic needs and priorities	Program M&E	—
		Amount of time spent (or travel distance) by women and girls to gather fuel or water for domestic use.	Basic needs and priorities	Program M&E, WHO Household Energy Database	2.1.4. Women and girls benefiting from new or improved infrastructure (number) and 2.4.1. Time-saving or gender-responsive infrastructure assets and/or services established or improved (number)
	Increased employment and entrepreneurship opportunities for women in the energy sector	Number of women whose economic activities reflect a move up the value chain and/or a shift into nontraditional subsectors.	Empowerment	Program M&E	2.1 Skilled jobs for women generated (number)
		Percentage of women in decision-making bodies (management, boards, committees) in the energy sector	Empowerment	Program M&E	2.3 Women represented in decision-making structures and processes (number) 2.3.1. Women with strengthened leadership capacities (number)

continued on next page

Table A1.4, *continued*

	Statement	Indicator	Level of Impact	Source	Corresponding ADB Tracking Indicator
Outcome		Number of human resource policies implemented aimed at attracting and retaining women employees	Shifting institutions and cultural and social norms	Program M&E	2.3.2 Measures on gender equality supported in implementation (number)
Output	Wider range of energy tariff and payment options available for women e.g., cheaper off-peak pricing options, payments in installments, flexible tariff structures provided for female-headed households and women-owned enterprises	Number of energy tariffs or payment schemes informed by the needs of women developed and implemented	Basic needs and priorities	Program M&E	2.4.1 Time-saving or gender-responsive infrastructure assets and/or services established or improved (number) 2.1.4
	More women are connected to the energy grid including female-headed households and women-owned enterprises	Number and proportion of men/boys and women/girls with access to reliable and affordable electricity (and other energy services)	Basic needs and priorities	Program M&E, service providers, World Energy Outlook electricity access database	2.1.4. Women and girls benefiting from new or improved infrastructure (number)
	Off-grid energy products and solutions available better suit the needs of women including opportunities for women as operators and energy entrepreneurs	Percentage of women with primary reliance on off-grid clean fuels and technology for cooking	Basic needs and priorities	ESCAP Online Statistical Database	2.1.4 Women and girls benefiting from new or improved infrastructure (number)
	Strengthened institutional capacity to address women's energy needs including the ability to collect sex-disaggregated data and use it for evidence-based decision-making	Percentage of staff in energy institutions who perceive they can address women's energy needs	Shifting institutions and cultural and social norms	Program M&E	

continued on next page

Table A1.4, *continued*

	Statement	Indicator	Level of Impact	Source	Corresponding ADB Tracking Indicator
Output	More women are trained in energy management training including skills for employment in the energy supply chain, for example in sales, marketing, and distribution of new products and services.	Number of women in energy companies enrolled in technical, management, and skills development training	Empowerment	Program M&E	2.3.1 Women with strengthened leadership capacities (number)
	More women are employed in the project's energy infrastructure construction including women from areas local to infrastructure investments	Number of women employed in project's energy infrastructure construction, disaggregated by geographical area of residence	Empowerment	Program M&E	2.1. Skilled jobs for women generated (number)

ESCAP = Economic and Social Commission for Asia and the Pacific, M&E = monitoring and evaluation, WHO = World Health Organization.
Source: Compiled for this report.

Figure A1.1: ADB Strategy 2030 Operational Priority 2— Accelerating Progress in Gender Equality

Results Framework Indicators (RFIs) and Tracking Indicators (TIs)

Pillar 1. Women's economic empowerment increased

RFI	2.1	**Skilled jobs for women generated (number)**
TI	2.1.1	Women enrolled in TVET and other job training (number)
TI	2.1.2	Women opening new accounts (number)
TI	2.1.3	Women-owned or -led SME loan accounts opened or women-owned or -led SME end borrowers reached (number)
TI	2.1.4	Women and girls benefiting from new or improved infrastructure (number)

Pillar 2. Gender equality in human capital enhanced

RFI	2.2	**Women and girls completing secondary and tertiary education, and/or other training (number)**
TI	2.2.1	Women and girls enrolled in STEM or nontraditional TVET (number)
TI	2.2.2	Health services for women and girls established or improved (number)
TI	2.2.3	Solutions to prevent or address gender-based violence implemented (number)

Pillar 3. Women's participation in decision-making and leadership enhanced

RFI	2.3	**Women represented in decision-making structures and processes (number)**
TI	2.3.1	Women with strengthened leadership capacities (number)
TI	2.3.2	Measures on gender equality supported in implementation (number)

Pillar 4. Women's time poverty and drudgery reduced

RFI	2.4	**Women and girls with increased time savings (number)**
TI	2.4.1	Time-saving or gender-responsive infrastructure assets and/or services established or improved (number)
TI	2.4.2	Child and elderly care services established or improved (number)

Pillar 5. Women's resilience to external shocks strengthened

RFI	2.5	**Women and girls with increased resilience to climate change, disasters, and other external shocks (number)**
TI	2.5.1	Community-based initiatives to build resilience of women and girls to external shocks implemented (number)
TI	2.5.2	Climate- and disaster-resilient infrastructure assets and/or services for women and girls established or improved (number)
TI	2.5.3	Savings and insurance schemes for women implemented or established (number)
TI	2.5.4	Dedicated crisis-responding social assistance schemes for women and girls implemented or established (number)

Source: Compiled for this report.

CASE STUDIES

This annex presents six case studies to illustrate approaches highlighted in this paper. Case studies have been selected to reflect a mix of ADB and non-ADB financed projects, a range of geographies, stakeholders (private, sovereign, and civil society), and project approaches. The case studies illustrate key gender equality-related features incorporated in each program and key benefits where data on outcomes was available.

Case Study 1—GreenCell Electric Bus Financing Project

Lender:	ADB
Type:	Private Sector
Country:	India
Sectors:	Transport
Gender Classification:	Gender Equality Theme

Project Description

India's public transport needs are projected to experience rapid growth as the country undergoes urbanization. Public transport accounts for only 7% of total trips in India, significantly lower than the global average of 30% to 35%. Road transport dominates, accounting for 87% of all passenger trips, 18% of total energy consumption, and 11.7% of greenhouse gas emissions in 2020. To address these challenges and achieve ambitious climate change mitigation targets, India aims to transition to alternative means of transport and increase the use of public transport.

Improving access to safe and secure travel options is a crucial priority, particularly for women in India. Studies indicate that women often feel unsafe and vulnerable when using public transport, sometimes even choosing to drop out of the labor force or education because of the lack of safe commuting options. Measures to enhance transport safety such as adequate lighting and the presence of marshals and surveillance tools, have been implemented by state governments. Building on these efforts, the project aims to incorporate gender-responsive measures into privately operated bus transportation. The Asian Development Bank (ADB) is collaborating with (GreenCell Mobility Private Limited [GMPL]) to implement a gender action plan that promotes gender equality and women's empowerment by enhancing safety and security features in transportation and providing leadership training for women staff.

Design and Monitoring Framework Outcomes and Outputs	
Outcomes	Operation of green and safer-for-women transportation systems in India expanded
Outputs	(i) Development and operation of e-buses in a gender-sensitive manner.
	(ii) Generation of local employment opportunities.
	(iii) Enhancement of gender equality in employment opportunities and working conditions at GMPL.

Key Gender-Related Project Features

- Conducted a women's safety audit to assess the operationalization of safety measures.
- Installed women-friendly safety features in all GreenCell Express Private Limited vehicles and bus depots.
- Provided safety response protocol training to all bus drivers and cabin hosts, with specific attention to women passengers' safety.
- Implemented a women's leadership program at GMPL.
- Recruited female interns for technical positions in GMPL's internship program.
- Hosted awareness-raising activities on gender inclusive initiatives and practices, covering women's safety features in vehicles, gender equality at work, and zero tolerance for sexual harassment, for GMPL's staff, contractors, and business partners.
- Submitted periodic reports on the implementation of gender measures to ADB.
- Qualified for 2X gender financing tag, meeting the eligibility criteria for 2X gender financing.

Source: ADB. 2022c. *India: GreenCell Electric Bus Financing Project*. Manila.

Case Study 2—Livable Cities Investment Project for Balanced Development

Lender:	ADB
Type:	Sovereign
Country:	Georgia
Sectors:	Water, Urban, and Sanitation; Agriculture, Natural Resources, and Rural Development; Transport
Gender Classification:	Effective Gender Mainstreaming

Project Description

The Livable Cities Investment Project for Balanced Development is a loan project totaling €101 million. It aims to improve livability and foster economic growth in Georgia, including the lagging regions and the capital city. The project targets at least 1.5 million people (52% women). It focuses on implementing integrated urban solutions to create inclusive and climate-resilient infrastructure and services. This includes upgrading urban centers, public spaces, parks, and community infrastructure, as well as restoring cultural and natural heritage sites. The project also prioritizes enhancing road infrastructure and connectivity. To ensure equal access and benefits, the project applies universal design, accessibility standards, and gender-responsive design principles.

Design and Monitoring Framework Outcomes and Outputs

Outcomes	Livability and inclusive economic activity in Georgia improved.
Outputs	(i) Inclusive and climate-resilient urban infrastructure rehabilitated and constructed, and services improved.
	(ii) Improved accessibility, connectivity, and mobility in tourism clusters across Georgia.
	(iii) Enhanced institutional capacity for sustainable urban and regional development.

Highlighted Gender-Related Project Features

- **Addressing gender issues in urban infrastructure planning:** This included city center upgrading following gender-sensitive features from the Inclusive Cities: Urban Area Guidelines approved by the Government of Georgia in 2020, and gender-responsive guidelines to ensure safe mobility and accessibility for women and girls.
- **Incorporation of gender-sensitive facilities:** This included gender design features such as separate male and female toilets; well-lit and child-friendly waiting spaces for parents and toddlers; safety signs that include emergency numbers and reporting authorities posted inside and outside the buildings of kindergartens, libraries, and sports complexes; and walkways, sidewalks, and with pram and wheelchair ramps, incorporated in the construction and rehabilitation of kindergartens, libraries, and sports complexes.
- **Mainstreaming of gender in public transport and other services:** This included printed information on gender-based violence and sexual harassment, including reporting protocols and hotlines, distributed at the entrance of cultural and heritage sites.
- Additional gender mainstreaming activities included:
  - o Supporting micro, small, and medium-sized enterprises headed by women
  - o Strengthening the role of gender equality councils
  - o Conducting capacity building for female staff
  - o Introducing gender-sensitive tools and strategies for implementing agencies

Key Learnings and Benefits

While evaluations of this project are not yet available, it highlights the adoption of key gender mainstreaming features in the development of urban spaces, as well as several causal pathways outlined in this paper. For example:

- Design codes and guidance on gender-inclusive infrastructure informed the construction of new public facilities. These public facilities will be more accessible to parents, children, and older people.
- The program aims to provide access to gender-based violence and harassment services and reporting, as well as awareness raising. This addresses key safety concerns related to incidents in public facilities.
- The program aims to build the capacity of institutions to address gender equality in future infrastructure design, including through direct representation, training, and introduction of strategies and tools.

Source: ADB. 2021. *Georgia: Livable Cities Investment Project for Balanced Development Project*. Manila.

A2.3: Case Study 3—Flood Emergency Reconstruction and Resilience Project

Lender:	ADB
Type:	Sovereign
Country:	Pakistan
Sectors:	Transport
Gender Classification:	Effective Gender Mainstreaming

Project Description

The Flood Emergency Reconstruction and Resilience Project was initiated in response to the request from the Government of Pakistan. The Asian Development Bank (ADB) approved a loan of $218.04 million and provided technical assistance of $2 million for the project in 2015. The project aimed to restore and reconstruct critical public and social infrastructure to multi-hazard resilience standards. The key project outputs included the reconstruction of flood-damaged roads and bridges in Punjab and Haveli, Kotli, and Poonch districts (HKP), the implementation of flood-resilient irrigation and flood management infrastructure in Punjab, and the strengthening of disaster risk management efforts.

Design and Monitoring Framework Outcomes and Outputs	
Outcomes	Restoration and reconstruction of critical public and social infrastructure to multi-hazard resilience standards
Outputs	(i) Reconstruction of flood-damaged roads and bridges in Punjab and Haveli, Kotli, and Poonch districts
	(ii) Implementation of flood-resilient irrigation and flood management infrastructure in Punjab
	(iii) Strengthening of disaster risk management

Key Gender-Related Project Features:

- Increased women's participation in community consultation and awareness-raising activities
- Inclusion of safety measures and consideration of commuter and pedestrian concerns in the design of roads and bridges (as part of the "Build Back Better" approach)
- Encouragement of contractors to include women under cash-for-work schemes for unskilled labor, based on women's willingness to work
- Addressing women's grievances and concerns during reconstruction work
- Employment of women in planting and maintaining plants along irrigation channels and protection bunds
- Improvement of women's income through participation in landslide risk mitigation measures
- Collection of sex-disaggregated data under the multi-hazard risk assessment
- Ensuring a gender-inclusive awareness campaign in disaster risk reduction, preparedness, and response
- Recruitment of social development and gender specialists at project coordination units

- Capacity building of implementing agencies in gender-inclusive project design and implementation
- Encouragement of recruitment of women staff in project implementation units
- Inclusion of gender action plan indicators in periodic reports and project monitoring system

Opportunities to Expand Gender Outcomes

The Flood Emergency Reconstruction and Resilience Project provides opportunities to expand gender outcomes through the inclusion of key gender-related project features. These features include increased women's participation in community consultation and awareness-raising activities, incorporating safety measures and commuters' and pedestrians' concerns in the design of roads and bridges, encouraging the inclusion of women under cash-for-work schemes, addressing women's grievances during reconstruction work, employing women in planting and maintaining plants, improving women's income through participation in landslide risk mitigation measures, collecting sex-disaggregated data, ensuring a gender-inclusive awareness campaign, recruiting social development and gender specialists, building capacity in gender-inclusive project design and implementation, encouraging the recruitment of women staff, and incorporating gender action plan indicators in monitoring and reporting.

Source: ADB. 2021. *Pakistan: Flood Emergency Reconstruction and Resilience Project*. Manila.

Case Study 4—Promoting Women's Employment in District Heating Projects

Lender:	European Bank of Reconstruction and Development, supported by funding from the Clean Technology Fund, a multi-donor trust fund established as part of the Climate Investment Fund.
Type:	Private Sector
Country:	Kazakhstan
Sectors:	Energy

Project Description

In countries like Kazakhstan—where long, cold winters are common—heating holds immense significance. Accessible and cost-effective heating both at homes and workplaces is a fundamental requirement, especially for individuals spending increased time indoors because of age or disabilities. Heating systems also play a vital role in generating employment opportunities. Enhancing heating efficiency stands as a priority, involving central district heating systems and localized boilers on the supply side, along with more energy-efficient construction on the demand side.

The primary aim of the study was to perform gender assessments for three projects, examining potential gender-related aspects and priorities linked to district heating and other heating sources. These assessments, conducted in 2014 in Aktau, Kyzylorda, and Semei, revealed that male employees comprised 70%–90% of the workforce in the district heating companies across these cities. Technical roles were predominantly held by men, while women were primarily employed in administrative positions connected to customer relations, accounting, and dispatch. Certain nontechnical departments were headed by women, while top management positions were primarily occupied by men.

Gender Equality Features

- To address this gender imbalance in terms of employment, the company gave priority to female technical students to access internship opportunities in the company, building on its agreements with technical training institutions on student internships. Additionally, the company paid the study fees of seven students, four of whom were female.
- The district heating company in Aktau adopted a gender-sensitive employment strategy after learning that most female customers were not happy to open their doors to male employees visiting their homes to read meters. As a result of these findings, women were employed to visit households for meter readings to conduct cost estimates and for collection of utility payments.

Key Benefits

Accessing gender-sensitive information through sex-disaggregated data and analysis enabled the company to improve its customer service. Meeting customer needs and preferences, and recognizing women as key customers, contributed to operational efficiency and high levels of customer service.

Supporting women's education and vocational training and then employment in science, technology, engineering, and mathematics (STEM) fields supports the possibilities of a more diverse workforce at all levels of an organization helping to meet the practical and strategic needs of the company, its employees, and the customers.

Sources: European Bank for Reconstruction and Development. 2014. *Gender Assessment of District Heating Projects in Kazakhstan financed by the Clean Technology Fund* (CTF). European Bank for Reconstruction and Development (EBRD) and Climate Investment Funds (CIF). 2016. *Gender Mainstreaming in District Heating Projects in the Commonwealth of Independent States: A Toolkit.*

Case Study 5—Community-Based Flood Management Program

Lender:	International Federation of Red Cross and Red Crescent Societies
Type:	Civil Society
Country:	Bangladesh
Sectors:	Climate

Project Description

In Bangladesh, women are particularly susceptible to disasters. It was found that following the 1991 cyclone, 90% of fatalities were women. This was because cultural norms required women to have a male relative with them in public shelters, resulting in many women and children perishing at home while awaiting a male relative's evacuation decision. Additionally, traditional clothing hindered women's ability to escape floods, and limited swimming skills further exacerbated the situation.

To address this issue, the Bangladesh Red Crescent Society initiated the Community-Based Disaster Management Flood and Earthquake Preparedness and Response Programme (CBDM) in 2005. This program aimed to reduce disaster vulnerability among people, particularly women, and enhance the preparedness of high-risk communities. Concentrating on flood and earthquake-prone regions, the initiative aimed to benefit 31,000 families across 80 communities in 10 flood-prone districts. The program focused on forming local disaster readiness groups, promoting awareness about disaster risks, constructing minor mitigation structures like tube wells, and enhancing livelihood opportunities.

Gender Equality Features

This program adopted several gender equality features in its delivery. General design features included the following:

- Integration of sex-segregated data within reporting systems
- Establishment of recruitment targets, with 50% for female participants in community disaster management committees, and 30% for community disaster response teams
- Conducting essential first aid and disaster risk reduction training for both women and men, along with tailored courses such as traditional birth attendant training for women based on self-identified needs and priorities
- Considering gender-specific vulnerabilities when devising and executing disaster mitigation strategies
- Implementing livelihood support initiatives catering to distinct requirements of men and women: sewing machines for women and 3-wheeler rickshaws for men
- Incorporating local political and religious leaders as volunteers in addressing cultural and religious barriers to women's involvement.

Needs Assessment and Vulnerability Targeting

The program adopted needs and vulnerability assessments to assist in tailoring interventions. When a community is chosen to participate in the CBDM program, the initial evaluation of the area incorporates gender- and age-specific data collected through field visits and surveys. Women are involved in the assessment team, although not typically in an equal ratio to men.

Following the initial evaluation, vulnerability and capacity assessments are conducted. This process allows both local men and women to assess their situations based on personal experiences. They then prioritize their requirements and create community action plans. During these assessments, local leaders and volunteers acknowledged that certain women and children faced elevated vulnerability to disaster impacts, including those in single-parent households because of divorce or widowhood. The design process gave special attention to addressing the needs of these groups.

Key Benefits and Lessons Learned

- The effectiveness of CBDM disaster risk reduction interventions is evident in the Bangladesh Red Crescent Society's prompt and efficient response to floods. Furthermore, the impact of floods was less severe in CBDM areas compared to nonparticipating regions.
- Achieving a balanced ratio of male-to-female volunteers at 50:50 and advancing women into leadership roles has notably enhanced women's access to CBDM program benefits. This approach guarantees the integration of women's perspectives and needs into planning, ultimately bolstering women's and their families' primary health care, livelihoods, and survival strategies. This results in an improved quality of life, heightened disaster readiness, and elevated hygiene standards. The establishment of targets and quotas, alongside related promotional tactics, has been instrumental in recruiting more female volunteers.

➡ The engagement of local political, community, and religious leaders significantly influences effective program execution within the community, including fostering acceptance of women's participation.

Source: International Federation of Red Cross and Red Crescent Societies. 2010. *A Practical Guide to Gender-sensitive Approaches for Disaster Management*.

Case Study 6—Women's Leadership in the Banda Golra Water Supply Scheme, Pakistan

Lender:	Sarhad Rural Support Programme (SRSP) (Regional NGO)
Country:	Pakistan
Sectors:	Water, Sanitation, and Hygiene

Project Description

The Banda Golra Water Supply Scheme in Pakistan aimed to address the long-standing challenges faced by the village regarding water access and sanitation. The village, consisting of about 120 households, had limited water sources and inadequate infrastructure. The project was initiated and led by Nasim Bibi, who formed a community-based women's organization (CBO) in 2002 to access credit from the SRSP. With the support of the SRSP, CBO members implemented a savings scheme and obtained loans to fund the installation of seven new hand pumps in locations throughout the village. The project involved active participation from both women and men in the community and aimed to improve water access, sanitation, health, women's empowerment, education, and community involvement.

Gender Equality Features

➡ Inclusive financial opportunities: The CBO members initiated a savings scheme, enabling women to access loans from the SRSP. Over 2 years, 21 women received loans and successfully repaid them. This financial inclusion empowered women economically and enhanced their decision-making power within their households.

➡ Women's active involvement and knowledge of community needs: During the monthly CBO meetings, women identified the need for improved water access as a priority and took the initiative to develop a village water supply scheme. This active involvement demonstrated women's leadership and their ability to identify and address community needs.

➡ Women's leadership: Nasim Bibi played a crucial role as a community leader and served as the project manager for the water scheme. Her leadership inspired other women to become involved as community leaders. The formation of three committees, managed predominantly by women, showcased their organizational and management skills in driving the project's success.

➡ Active participation in project activities: Women actively contributed to the implementation of the project. They assisted in softening the ground for drilling and participated in the construction of hand pump platforms. This hands-on involvement showcased women's capabilities in physical labor and their commitment to improving water access in the village.

⊘ Collaborative efforts: Every participating household took turns providing food and accommodation for the laborers engaged in hand pump drilling. This collective effort demonstrated the community's recognition of the importance of the water scheme and their willingness to support its implementation. The inclusive nature of the project fostered a sense of unity and shared responsibility among community members.

Key Learnings and Benefits

⊘ Improved Sanitation and Health: The availability of clean water resulted in increased bathing frequency, better clothes-washing practices, and reduced contamination of water sources. This positively impacted the overall health and hygiene of the community.

⊘ Time Savings and Productive Use: The implementation of the water supply scheme resulted in a significant decrease in the time required for collecting water, freeing up valuable hours for women and girls. Women reported using this extra time for family and group meetings, allowing for increased social interaction and community engagement. Girls, on the other hand, utilized the additional time for embroidery and sewing, developing skills that benefited themselves and their families.

⊘ Women's Empowerment and Recognition: Through their involvement in the water and credit schemes, women experienced increased decision-making power at the household level. They were also recognized for their effectiveness as community leaders. Women were able to openly discuss health issues, including family planning, leading to a greater sense of empowerment.

⊘ Enhanced Social Mobility and Independence: Women experienced greater social mobility, both within and outside their homes. They developed social relationships beyond their immediate households, fostering a sense of independence and empowerment.

⊘ Improved Education: The project led to an improvement in girls' access to education. The establishment of a nonformal school in the village provided primary and secondary education opportunities, primarily for girls.

⊘ Community Involvement and Participation: The project led to increased community involvement and participation. The number of CBO members significantly increased, and male family members began to support and perceive the project as a collective effort benefiting the entire community.

⊘ Some key factors of success can be drawn from this example, including:

⊘ Trust and support in the community: The success of the credit scheme, along with familial relationships, helped build trust and support among the community members, facilitating the acceptance of the water scheme.

⊘ The importance of engaging men, male involvement, and support: The active involvement of male family members and the engagement of men in shared management models contributed to the success of the project. It helped in gaining support for the water supply scheme from the entire community.

⊘ Financial independence: Women's increased financial contributions to their families through the micro-credit scheme garnered respect and decision-making power within households and communities, strengthening their roles as community leaders.

Source: United Nations. 2006. *Gender, Water and Sanitation: Case Studies on Best Practices*.

REFERENCES

2X Climate Finance Taskforce. 2021. *Ways to Gender-Smart Climate Finance: Sustainable Cities*. 2X Collaborative, 2X Climate Finance Taskforce, CDC Group plc, European Investment Bank (EIB), and European Bank for Reconstruction and Development (EBRD).

Adam Smith International. 2021. *Embedding Inclusivity into Infrastructure Development*.

L. Adams and L. Sorkin. 2016. *Empower Women, Build Resilience*. The Rockefeller Foundation.

B.E. Akineyemi et al. 2018. *Factors Explaining Household Payment for Potable Water in South Africa. Cogent Social Sciences*. 4(1).

P. Alstone et al. 2011. *Expanding Women's Role in Africa's Modern Off-Grid Lighting Market*.

ARUP. 2022. *Cities Alive: Designing Cities that Work for Women*.

Asian Development Bank (ADB). 2013a. *Gender Tool Kit: Transport*. Manila.

————. 2013b. *Tip Sheet: Gender-Inclusive Approaches in Urban Development*. Manila.

————. 2015a. *Balancing the Burden? Desk Review of Women's Time Poverty and Infrastructure in Asia and the Pacific*. Manila.

————. 2015b. *Policy Brief: A Safe Public Transportation Environment for Women and Girls*. Manila.

————. 2018. *Tip Sheet: Gender-Inclusive Approaches in the Energy Sector*. Manila.

————. 2019. *Gender in Infrastructure: Lessons from Central and West Asia*. Manila.

————. 2022a. *Accelerating Gender Equality in the Renewable Energy Sector*. Manila.

————. 2022b. *Safer Trains: Expanding Communication Platforms to Report Gender-Based Violence in Transport Services in the Philippines*. Manila.

————. 2022c. *Regional: Integrating Gender and Social Inclusion Dimensions in Climate Change Interventions in Southeast Asia*. Manila.

M.H. Bhuiyan. 2013. Improving Women's Odds in Disasters. *World Bank News*. 12 December.

S. Biegel and S. Lambin. 2021. *Gender and Climate Investment: A strategy for unlocking a sustainable future*. Gender Smart.

F. Bonnet et al. 2021. *Home-based Workers in the World: A Statistical Profile*. WIEGO Statistical Brief No. 27. January.

British International Investment. n.d. *Sector Profiles: Infrastructure*.

Business and Sustainable Development Commission. 2017. *Better Business, Better World*.

M. Campbell. 2014. *Gender, income, and transportation mobility in Bangalore's IT sector*. Paper prepared for the 5th International Conference on Women's Issues in Transportation. Paris. April 14–16.

C. Carr. 2019. For street vendors, finding water and toilets isn't just a nuisance, it's cutting into earnings. *Women in Informal Employment: Globalizing and Organizing (WIEGO) Blog*.

M.A. Chen. 2014. *Informal Economy Monitoring Study Sector Report: Home-Based Workers*. Cambridge, MA, USA: WIEGO.

Council of Europe. 2009. *Gender budgeting: practical implementation Handbook*.

T. Dinkelman. 2011. The Effects of Rural Electrification on Employment: New Evidence from South Africa. *American Economic Review*. 101(7). pp. 3078–3108.

A. Erman et al. 2021. *Gender Dimensions of Disaster Risk and Resilience*. Washington, DC: World Bank.

European Commission, Directorate-General for Mobility and Transport. 2018. *Business Case to Increase Female Employment in Transport Business Case to Increase Female Employment In Transport – Final Report*.

European Parliament, Directorate General for Internal Policies. 2012. *The role of women in the green economy: the issue of mobility*. Brussels.

FP Analytics. 2020. *Women as Levers of Change: Unleashing the Power of Women to Transform Male-Dominated Industries*.

E. Fraser et al. 2017. *Violence against Women and Girls, Infrastructure and Cities. Briefing Paper*. Government of the United Kingdom, Infrastructure and Cities for Economic Development (ICED).

M. Grant et al. 2019. *Gender Equality and Goal 6 – The Critical Connection: An Australian Perspective*. Canberra: Australian Water Partnership.

S. Habtezion. 2012. *Gender and energy*. New York: United Nations Development Programme.

M. Hislop. 2021. Melinda Gates tells governments to think about childcare as "essential infrastructure". *Women's Agenda*. 28 January.

A. Hoeffler and J. Fearon. 2015. *Benefits and Costs of the Conflict and Violence Targets for the Post-2015 Development Agenda*. Conflict and Violence Assessment Paper. Copenhagen Consensus Center.

G. Hutton. 2015. Benefits and Costs of the Water, Sanitation and Hygiene Targets for the post-2015 Development Agenda. Post-2015 Consensus. Working Paper. Copenhagen Consensus Center.

Infrastructure and Cities for Economic Development (ICED). 2017. Promoting Women's Empowerment through Energy. *ICED Evidence Library*. ECDEV001.

International Federation of Red Cross and Red Crescent Societies. 2010. *A Practical Guide to Gender-sensitive Approaches for Disaster Management*.

International Finance Corporation (IFC). 2018. *Off-Grid Solar Market Trends Report 2018*. Washington, DC: World Bank.

———. 2019. *Gender Equality, Infrastructure and PPPs: A Primer*. Washington, DC: World Bank.

———. 2020. *Integrating Gender in Cities Projects*. Washington, DC: World Bank.

International Labour Organization. 2017. *World Employment and Social Outlook: Trends for Women 2017*. Geneva: International Labour Organization.

International Union for Conservation of Nature (n.d.) *Disaster and Gender Statistics*.

C. Jasper et al. 2012. Water and Sanitation in Schools: a systematic review of the health and educational outcomes. *International Journal of Environmental Research and Public Health*. 9(8). pp. 2272–2287.

Landesa. 2012. *Issue Brief: Women's Secure Rights to Land: Benefits, Barriers, and Best Practices*.

N.R. Libertun de Duren. 2017. The social housing burden: comparing households at the periphery and the center of cities in Brazil, Colombia, and Mexico. *International Journal of Housing Policy*. 18(2). pp. 177–203.

E. Lind. 2020. Gender equality, climate change and transportation. *URBACT*. 16 October.

McKinsey Global Institute. 2015. *The Power of Parity: How Advancing Women's Equality can add $12 Trillion to Global Growth*.

J. Menon. 2019. *Guide on Integrating Gender Throughout Infrastructure Project Phases in Asia and the Pacific*.

R. Mohun and S. Biswas. 2016. *Infrastructure: A Game-Changer for Women's Economic Empowerment*. Background paper for the UN Secretary-General's High Level Panel on Women's Economic Empowerment. November.

G. Morgan et al. 2020. *Infrastructure for gender equality and the empowerment of women*. Copenhagen, Denmark: UNOPS.

M. Munoz-Raskin et al. 2017. Women on the march! Two decades of gender inclusion in rural roads in Peru. *World Bank Blogs*. 26 June.

K. O'Dell et al. 2014. Women, energy and economic empowerment: Applying a gender lens to amplify the impact of energy access. *Deloitte Insights*. 19 September.

Office of the United Nations High Commissioner for Human Rights. 2012. *Women and the Right to Adequate Housing*.

M.B. Orlando et al. 2018. *Getting to Gender Equality in Energy Infrastructure: Lessons from Electricity Generation, Transmission, and Distribution Projects*. Energy Sector Management Assistance Program (ESMAP) Technical Report 012/18. Washington, DC: World Bank.

Organisation for Economic Co-operation and Development (OECD). 2019. Sustainable Connectivity: Closing the Gender Gap in Infrastructure. *OECD Environment Policy Paper* No. 15.

_____. 2021. Women in Infrastructure: Selected Stocktaking of Good Practices for Inclusion of Women in Infrastructure. *OECD Public Governance Policy Paper* No. 07.

_____. 2023. OECD Best Practices for Gender Budgeting. *OECD Journal on Budgeting*. 2023(1).

_____. 2023. *Gender equality in times of crisis: SIGI 2023 Global report*. Social Institutions and Gender Index.

Pacific Region Infrastructure Facility (PRIF). 2022. *Inclusive Infrastructure in the Pacific: Study on Gender Equality and Social Inclusion*.

D. Peters. 2013. *Gender and Sustainable Urban Mobility*. Official Thematic Study for the 2013 UN Habitat Global Report on Human Settlements.

Reall. 2021. *Safe and Secure Affordable Housing Communities for Women and Girls: Key Learnings and Recommendations in Africa and Asia*.

S. Roever. 2014. *Informal Economy Monitoring Study Sector Report: Street Vendors*. Cambridge, MA, USA: WIEGO.

A.V. Shankar et al. 2021. *Understanding Impacts of Women's Engagement in the Improved Cookstove Value Chain in Kenya: Executive Summary*. Global Alliance for Clean Cookstoves.

Shell Foundation. 2018. *A Business First Approach to Gender Inclusion: How to Think about Gender Inclusion in Small and Medium Enterprise Operations*.

The Solutions Lab. 2020. *Gender-Responsive Infrastructure: Thematic Brief*.

Sustainable Infrastructure Tool Navigator. n.d. *Gender-Responsive Infrastructure: How Inclusive Infrastructure Development Contributes to Equal Opportunities and Benefits*.

Taskar Center for Accessible Technology. n.d. *OpenSidewalks Project*.

K. Thompson et al. 2017. Thirsty for change: the untapped potential of women in urban water management. *Deloitte Insights*. 23 January.

A.M. Thurston et al. 2021. Natural hazards, disasters and violence against women and girls: a global mixed-methods systematic review. *BMJ Global Health*. 2021(6):e004377.

United Nations (UN). 2015. *The World's Women 2015: Trends and Statistics*. New York: UN, Department of Economic and Social Affairs, Statistics Division. Sales No. E.15.XVII.8

UN Human Settlements Programme (UN-Habitat). 2012. *Gender Issue Guide: Housing and Slum Upgrading*. Nairobi: UN-Habitat.

———. 2014. *Women and Housing: Towards Inclusive Cities*. Nairobi: UN-Habitat.

———. 2021. *Building Gender Inclusive Cities: Toward more Gender-Inclusive Programmes, Public Spaces and Cities in the Arab Region*.

UN-Water. 2006. *Gender, Water and Sanitation: A Policy Brief*. June.

UN Women. 2014. Making markets safer for women vendors in Papua New Guinea. *News story*. 14 April.

UN Women and UNOPS. 2019. *Guide on Integrating Gender into Infrastructure Development in Asia and the Pacific*.

UN Women Fiji. 2014. *Why is climate change a gender issue?*

United Nations Environment Programme. 2020. *Powering Equality: Women's Entrepreneurship Transforming Asia's Energy Sector*.

United Nations High Commissioner for Refugees (UNHCR). 2008. *UNHCR Handbook for the Protection of Women and Girls*. Geneva: Office of the United Nations High Commissioner for Refugees.

J. Vanek et al. 2014. Statistics on the Informal Economy: Definitions, Regional Estimates and Challenges. *WIEGO Working Paper* (Statistics) No. 2. April.

M. Waqar. 2021. Mainstreaming Gender in Infrastructure: Desk Review.

Water and Sanitation for the Urban Poor (WSUP). 2019. Gender balance in the water and sanitation workforce. *Blog*. 7 March.

Where Women Work. 2022. EIB cites the case for making transport solutions work for women. *Insight*. 2 August.

World Bank. 2015. *Violence Against Women and Girls: Transport Brief*.

———. 2019. Women in Water Utilities: Breaking Barriers. *World Bank News*. 27 August.

_____. 2020. *Handbook for Gender-Inclusive Urban Planning and Design*. Washington, DC: World Bank.

_____. 2021. *Women, Business and the Law 2021*. Washington, DC: World Bank.

World Health Organisation (WHO) and UNICEF. 2017. *Progress on Drinking Water, Sanitation and Hygiene: 2017 Update and SDG Baseliness*. Geneva: World Health Organization (WHO) and the United Nations Children's Fund (UNICEF).

A. Yepez. 2023. Gender equality: a pillar for sustainable infrastructure. *Blog*. Inter-American Development Bank (IDB). 31 January.

www.ingramcontent.com/pod-product-compliance
Lightning Source LLC
Chambersburg PA
CBHW061221270326
41926CB00032B/4802